WILD GUIDE

plants &
animals
of the Australian Alps

Barbara Cameron-Smith

Envirobook

First published in 1999 by Envirobook
38 Rose Street, Annandale NSW 2038
Phone. 02 9518 6154, Fax. 02 9518 6156
in association with the Australian Alps Liaison Committee

The National Library of Australia Cataloguing-in-Publication data
Cameron-Smith, Barbara
WILDGUIDE plants & animals of the Australian Alps

1st ed.
Includes index.

ISBN 0 85881 168 5

1. Natural history - Australian Alps (N.S.W. and Vic.)
2. Mountain animals - Australia - Australian Alps (N.S.W. and Vic.)
3. Botany - Australia - Australian Alps (N.S.W. and Vic.)
4. Zoology Australia - Australian Alps (N.S.W. and Vic.) I. Australian Alps Liaison
Committee. II. Australian Alps National Parks. III. Title. IV. Title; WILDGUIDE plants
& animals of the Australian Alps

Concept, research, text and photo research Barbara Cameron-Smith

Designer Jacqueline Richards

Photographs As individually credited, with special thanks to Colin Totterdell
who provided many of the flora photos.

Illustrations Barbara Cameron-Smith

Project coordination Ann Jelinek

Additional research Community Relations working group of the Australian Alps
Liaison Committee, and Mark Lintermans, Environment ACT.

Film Separation Pica Limited, Singapore

Printing and Binding Toppan Printing Company Hong Kong Limited

Paper 128 gsm Kinmari gloss art

Front cover *Gang-gang cockatoo* Photograph by J P Ferrero / Auscape
Billy buttons Photograph by J P Ferrero / Auscape
Mount Kosciuszko area in spring Photograph by T Acker / Auscape

Title page *Snow gums, Swindlers Spur, Alpine National Park* Photograph by
David Tatnall ©

Opposite *Spring thaw, Mount Kosciuszko region* Photograph by T Acker / Auscape

Back cover *Alpine mint-bush* Photograph by Colin Totterdelll
Common eastern froglet Photograph by G A Hoye / Nature focus

contents

A list of contacts for further information and useful maps can be found on the inside back cover.

Life On Top of AUSTRALIA

What's in this guide?

This booklet introduces you to animals and plants that are commonly seen or heard in the Australian Alps, plus a handful of threatened species. It also includes a small number of introduced and feral plants and animals that have an impact on native species.

Where can I use this guide?

The Australian Alps national parks—an almost 500 kilometre long stretch of the Great Dividing Range—comprises 1.6 million hectares of national parks and conservation reserves. The Alps parks include:
• Australian Capital Territory's Namadgi National Park
• New South Wales' Kosciuszko and Brindabella national parks, and Scabby Range and Bimberi nature reserves
• Victoria's Alpine, Snowy River and Mount Buffalo national parks, and the Avon Wilderness Park.

Many of the featured plants and animals can also be found in the ranges beyond the Australian Alps. So pack this guide when visiting:
• New South Wales' New England and Barrington Tops

PHOTOGRAPH J CANCALOSI / AUSCAPE

Red-necked wallaby

national parks, Mount Canobolas (near Orange), the Greater Blue Mountains and the Tinderry Range; and:
• Victoria's Mounts Buller, Hotham, Stirling, Skene, Baw Baw, Donna Buang, Falls Creek and Lake Mountain.

What's the best time?

Naturally, plants and animals are most visible during the snow-free months. Don't forget that reptiles, fish and insects are more likely to be out and about during the day. On the other hand, native mammals are usually active from dusk till dawn. Also keep in mind that flowering times vary from year to year. An early snowmelt brings forward flowering but if the snow lingers, flowering may be delayed for weeks.

Why can't I find it?

This wouldn't be a pocket guide if it covered every known plant or animal that lives in the Australian Alps national parks. Jot down details of species you can't find and ask at your nearest visitor centre or ranger station for help. Look for a selection of more comprehensive references on page 94.

Why hands off?

Your need to know the identity of a plant or animal must always take second place to its well-being. Avoid souveniring bits and pieces, getting too close, making undue noise, or trying to get a reaction out of wildlife. All native plants, animals and natural communities are protected.

How do I get there?

You'll get the most out of this guide if you use it together with maps and general guides available from various visitor information centres in the Australian Alps (details on inside back cover). For a comprehensive, practical guide and lasting memento of your visit, look out for 'Explore the Australian Alps: a touring guide to the Australian Alps national parks'.

How To
USE THIS GUIDE

OPTION ONE
FLIP THROUGH SHORTCUT

Turn to the plant or animal pages and flip through till you find the best photo match with the species you've spotted.

What's that animal?
Pages 26–55

Turn to the animal pages which are divided into Mammals; Birds; Reptiles; Frogs, Fish, Crayfish; and Insects & Spiders. For easy identification, the largest animal group—the Birds—have been grouped according to colour, for example, 'black' or 'brownish grey' birds. Within the colour groupings, the species are featured in order of decreasing size. Animal categories with fewer species, such as Reptiles, have been grouped according to similarity, and can be compared at a glance.

What's that plant?
Pages 56–93

Turn to the plant pages which are divided into Trees; Flowering Shrubs & Herbs; Sedges & Mosses; Ferns, and Grasses. To help identification, Flowering Shrubs & Herbs have been grouped according to flower colour and similarity. In the other categories, including 'Trees', the tallest species are listed first and shortest last.

OPTION TWO
HABITAT BACKTRACK

What's that Habitat?
Pages 16–25

To identify a species according to the habitat in which it occurs, turn to the Altitude-Habitat diagram on page 15. Identify which habitat you are in, turn to its summary page and check the listed plants and animals and the page on which they are featured.

What's a habitat?
A habitat is the basic set of living conditions that a plant or animal needs for survival. These include the right range of foods, shelter and climatic conditions. Specialised plants and animals may be confined to part of one habitat while more adaptable species thrive within a number of habitats. Species that move between habitats, for example wombats, have been listed wherever they occur to allow cross referencing.

INTRODUCED AND TREATENED PLANTS & ANIMALS

A small number of the species in this guide are highlighted because they are not native to Australia, having been brought here by European settlers. Some, such as rabbits and foxes, were introduced into the wild from the earliest days and are now known as 'introduced' species. Domesticated imports that escaped to fend for themselves, including cats and goats, are classed as 'feral'. Troublesome 'introduced' plants are sometimes termed 'weeds', including agricultural and ornamental imports that have encroached into natural areas. A few rarely seen plants and animals have been included because they are only found in the Australian Alps, and therefore deserve special mention. As their numbers are dwindling, and threats to their existence remain, they are classed as 'threatened'. 'Threatened' species includes 'endangered' species that are bordering on extinction, and 'vulnerable' species that are heading down that road. Consider yourself lucky if you see any plants or animals highlighted as 'threatened'.

5

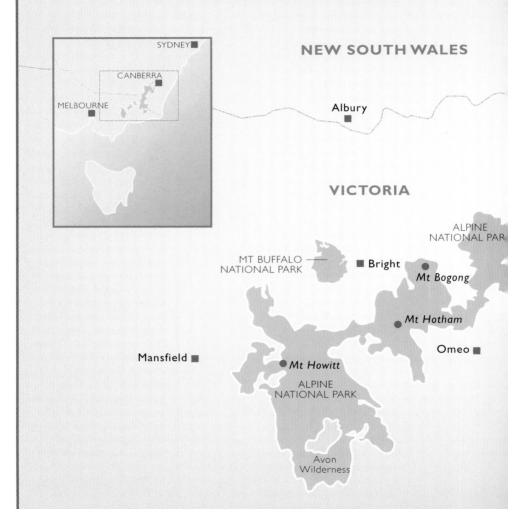

Australian Alps
NATIONAL PARKS

NEW SOUTH WALES

SYDNEY ▪

CANBERRA
▪

MELBOURNE
▪

Albury ▪

VICTORIA

ALPINE
NATIONAL PAR

MT BUFFALO ——
NATIONAL PARK

▪ Bright

● *Mt Bogong*

● *Mt Hotham*

Omeo ▪

Mansfield ▪

● *Mt Howitt*

ALPINE
NATIONAL PARK

Avon
Wilderness

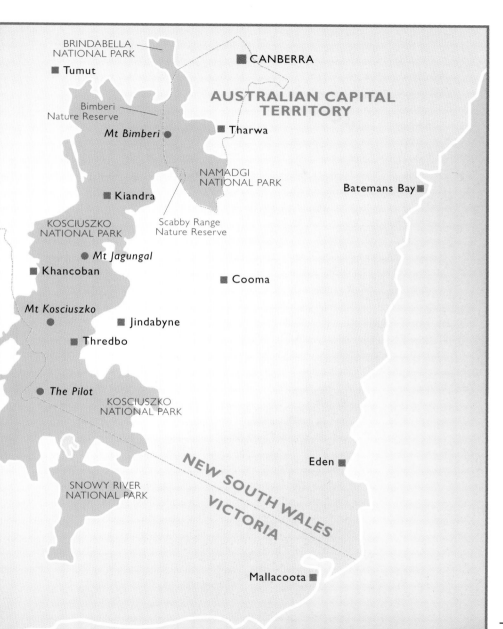

BRINDABELLA
NATIONAL PARK

■ Tumut

■ CANBERRA

AUSTRALIAN CAPITAL
TERRITORY

Bimberi
Nature Reserve

Mt Bimberi ●

■ Tharwa

NAMADGI
NATIONAL PARK

Batemans Bay ■

■ Kiandra

Scabby Range
Nature Reserve

KOSCIUSZKO
NATIONAL PARK

● *Mt Jagungal*

■ Khancoban

■ Cooma

Mt Kosciuszko
●

■ Jindabyne

■ Thredbo

● *The Pilot*

KOSCIUSZKO
NATIONAL PARK

NEW SOUTH WALES

Eden ■

SNOWY RIVER
NATIONAL PARK

VICTORIA

Mallacoota ■

7

Australian Alps
NATIONAL PARKS

The unique Australian Alps provide a stark contrast to the rest of the continent which is mainly flat and dry. Their rugged, mountainous ridges and high plains cross State and Territory borders, stretching from the outskirts of Canberra to the mountains of Victoria. The Australian Alps national parks protect 1.6 million hectares of this highest ground. Parks and reserves in the ACT's Brindabella Range, NSW's Snowy Mountains, and

Victoria's scattered mountains and plateaux contain plants and animals found nowhere else in the world. As well as protecting important Aboriginal and European heritage sites, they safeguard outstanding tourism and recreational opportunities, and the catchment areas of major rivers.

In 1986, national park authorities from NSW, Victoria, and the ACT, along with the Commonwealth Government, agreed to jointly manage this significant national asset. Cooperation and teamwork ensures that the parks and reserves in the Alps are managed as one biogeographic region.

To find out more information about this unique cross border management program, visit the Australian Alps national parks internet site at: **www.australianalps.environment.gov.au**

PHOTOGRAPH G ROBERTSON / AUSCAPE

Lake Cootapatamba, Kosciuszko National Park

AUSTRALIAN CAPITAL TERRITORY

Namadgi National Park
- 106 000 hectares

Initially declared in 1979, an expanded Gudgenby Nature Reserve became Namadgi National Park in 1984, safeguarding almost 45% of the ACT. Broad grassy valleys and tree-clad ridges lead up to the 1911 metre Bimberi Peak. Low open woodlands cover most of the park, with tall wet forests growing in sheltered locations, especially on wetter western slopes.

Namadgi's diverse habitats, ranging from open valleys to snow gum woodlands, support a wide variety of plants and animals, and the central Namadgi ranges are renowned for their bold granite outcrops. Namadgi National Park continues to be of great significance to local Aboriginal peoples. From the 1830s, pastoralists began to settle in the broad southern valleys. Cold air drainage and pastoral clearing created the treeless valleys on the eastern side of the park. These majestic valleys can be reached from the Naas and Boboyan Road which runs from the village of Tharwa, on the outskirts of Canberra, to Adaminaby in NSW.

The Cotter and Uriarra Roads head west from Canberra to the Brindabella Range via the Brindabella Road. Subalpine woodlands give way to heaths and stunted snow gums on the highest ridges and peaks which provide excellent views over the adjoining Kosciuszko National Park, and Namadgi and Tidbinbilla ranges. Rain and snowmelt stored in the subalpine sphagnum bogs feed into the Cotter River catchment which provides 85% of Canberra's water supply.

NEW SOUTH WALES

Kosciuszko National Park
• 650 000 hectares
After a lengthy battle to protect the largest portion of the Australian Alps, the Snowy Mountains of New South Wales were reserved in 1944 as Kosciusko State Park. Upgraded to a national park in 1967, the extended park conserves Australia's highest point, the 2228 metre Mount Kosciuszko, and a string of other peaks along the treeless Main Range. As the source of the Snowy and Upper Murray Rivers, the park is renowned for its diverse landforms, ranging from rounded granitic outcrops and glacial lakes to flat-topped mountains, limestone country and deep river valleys.

The northern section of the park, stretching from Tumut to Adaminaby, combines outstanding natural features such as Yarrangobilly Caves, with the legacy of past land uses, including gold mining centred on Kiandra. Dams and reservoirs constructed as part of the Snowy Mountains Scheme provide boating and fishing opportunities. In stark contrast are the drier pine-clad ridges of the Lower Snowy region which link up with Victoria's Snowy River National Park.

Scabby Range Nature Reserve
• 3449 hectares
Bimberi Nature Reserve
• 7100 hectares
The western border of Namadgi National Park is flanked by two nature reserves set aside for their conservation values and remoteness. Directly west of Namadgi, the Bimberi Nature Reserve is best viewed from the 1762 metre Mount Ginini at the end of the Mount Franklin Road. The Scabby Range Nature Reserve lies directly south of Namadgi's 1829 metre Mount Kelly and is only accessible to walkers.

Brindabella National Park
• 12 600 hectares
North-west of the NSW-ACT border, and 30 kilometres west of Canberra, the park conserves part of the steep forested Brindabella Range and helps protect the Coree Catchment

9

which feeds into the Cotter Catchment (and Canberra's water supply). Red stringybarks and scribbly gums abound, providing vital wildlife corridors between neighbouring parks and reserves. Higher up, snow gums and mountain gums clothe the 1421 metre Mount Coree, the park's high point. Four wheel drive tracks connect lookouts and provide access around this magnificent national park.

VICTORIA

Alpine National Park
• 646 000 hectares
Victoria's Alpine National Park consists of a series of high plains separated by deep valleys. In 1989, the Cobberas-Tingaringy, Wonangatta-Moroka and Bogong national parks were combined to create the Alpine National Park, forming a vital link in the Australian Alps national parks. The state's largest national park, it contains Victoria's high point, the 1986 metre Mount Bogong.

The Cobberas-Tingaringy area lies directly across the border from The Pilot and Lower Snowy in Kosciuszko National Park. To its west lie the Dartmouth area and spectacular Bogong High Plains, and Mount Feathertop. To the south-east, the rugged

PHOTOGRAPH BY DAVID TATNALL ©

The Alps from Victoria's Mount Buffalo

Wonnangatta-Moroka country offers challenging bushwalking and camping, with magnificent views from the 1742 metre Mount Howitt across the Crosscut Saw, The Razorback and The Bluff.

Mount Buffalo National Park
• 31 000 hectares
As early as 1898, Mount Buffalo's scenic and recreational values prompted the declaration of a national park. The steep-sided granite plateau provides year round recreational opportunities, including walking, camping, rock climbing, ski touring, tobogganing and hang gliding.

Snowy River National Park
• 98 100 hectares
The Snowy River National Park includes the spectacular Little River and Snowy River gorge which can be reached via the Barry Way from Jindabyne.

Avon Wilderness Park
• 39 650 hectares
Adjoining the Wonnangatta-Moroka area, the Avon Wilderness offers rugged walking and camping in trackless shining gum and mountain ash forests that give way to subalpine woodlands at higher altitudes.

Australian Alps
CLIMATE

For many Australians, seeing snow is a once in a life time experience. That's because 'snow country' on the mainland is confined to the Australian Alps national parks which occupy a mere 0.02% of the entire continent. Only 0.003% of Australia is truly alpine—unable to support tree growth. While our Alps are dwarfed by the towering peaks of New Zealand, Europe and the Himalayas, they still experience climatic extremes, including low temperatures, frequent frosts and strong winds. The Alps create their own weather by getting in the way of moisture-bearing clouds. Forced to rise, clouds cool and release their load of mist, rain, sleet or snow, depending on

PHOTOGRAPH BY DAVID TATNALL ©

The Cathedral, Mount Buffalo National Park

the temperatures. An average of 1800–2300 mm per year falls on the highest parts, with snow blanketing the subalpine and alpine zones for one to four months, and four to nine months a year, respectively.

In spring, the melting snows swell waterways, triggering local flooding. Summer promises a mixed bag of weather, including heatwaves, high winds, thunderstorms and freak snowfalls.

What to expect?
Don't forget that it's likely to be 10°C cooler above the tree line than in the foothills. It pays to be prepared for all seasons in one day, especially if leaving the car. The fact that temperatures drop with increasing altitude is not the only concern. The daily temperature range can vary up to 30°C in summer, especially when there's no cloud cover to trap heat. And because the air's thinner up top, the risk of ultraviolet sunburn soars.

PAST AND FUTURE CLIMATES

Over the millenia, the percentage of the continent annually snowed under has expanded and contracted in response to the fluctuating global climate. During cooler, wetter periods, Australia's highest ground (in present-day NSW and Tasmania) was exposed to periods of glaciation. Icecaps and slow-moving rivers of ice scraped, ground and gouged out solid rock and dammed waterways. Their legacy, including glacial lakes and moraines, can still be seen if you know what to look for, and where.

Scientists tell us that rising world-wide temperatures are contributing to the retreat of glaciers. While Australia has no permanent snow and ice, it is unlikely to escape the impacts of global warming. As temperatures rise, so will the tree line, encroaching on the unique treeless alpine tracts, and reducing the habitats of our truly alpine plants and animals.

Downwardly mobile
MOUNTAINS

With more than 10 peaks exceeding 2100 metres, the Australian Alps are a noteworthy landmark in a continent averaging just 300 metres above sea level. But by overseas standards, the Alps are 'vertically challenged'. At 2228 metres, Mount Kosciuszko is just over half the height of New Zealand's Mount Cook (3744 metres), and around a quarter the height of Mount Everest. There's a good reason for the differences in altitude. While New Zealand's Southern Alps are still being squeezed up by geological forces, the much older Australian Alps have been worn down by on-going weathering and erosion. Instead of angular alpine peaks rising out of deep valleys, rounded high points sit atop uplifted undulating ranges and plateaux. These high points are usually isolated rocky outcrops that have proved more resilient than surrounding rocks.

WHAT'S THAT ROCK TYPE?

GRANITE BOULDERS

Close-up Because granite cools slowly at depth, there is time to form big grainy crystals or minerals. Look for mega crystals in shades of white, grey, pink and black. Depending on the mineral mix, some granites appear mottled-grey while others are pinkish.

Large-grained granite

At a distance Look for outcrops of rounded or blocky boulders or tors, sometimes balancing on top of each other. Weathering and erosion widen the expansion cracks that form during underground cooling, or as overlying rocks are worn away, releasing pressure. These same cracks provide shelter from sunlight and snow for many plants and animals. Granite breaks down into a relatively nutrient-poor soil, with a sandy surface overlaying clay.

Where to see granite landforms?

ACT
- Square Rock
- Booromba Rocks
- Mount Gingera
- Orroral and Gudgenby valleys

NSW
- Thredbo Top Station
- Mount Kosciuszko
- Perisher Valley
- Charlotte Pass

VIC
- Mount Bogong
- Mount Buffalo
- Mount Baw Baw

Granite boulders,
Lake Cootapatamba.

PHOTOGRAPHY BY DAVID TATNALL ©

PHOTOGRAPHY BY DAVID TATNALL ©

BASALT COLUMNS

Ruined Castle, Bogong High Plains

Close-up Because basalt is created by lava flows, it cools quickly above ground into a fine-grained rock featuring dark grey to black, fine to medium crystals.

At a distance Look for flat-topped mountains and columns. Why? Valleys filled with basalt lava resist weathering better than the surrounding landscape, forming inverted 'bathtubs' of volcanic rock. During the cooling process, thick layers of lava crack into distinctive six-sided columns. Basalt weathers into a clay-rich soil that supports moisture-loving plants that thrive on fertile soils.

PHOTOGRAPH J BURT / A.N.T. PHOTO LIBRARY

Where to see basalt landforms?

ACT   No basalt landforms

NSW   • Tabletop Mountain
      • Round Mountain
      • Mount Jagungal

VIC   • Mount Loch
      • Mount Jim
      • Ruined Castle
      • Dargo High Plains

ICE AT WORK

Ice is a 'wrecker' when it comes to speeding up weathering and erosion in the Alps. *How does it work?* When water freezes it expands. At the macro level, moisture collected in cracks, expands and wedges the rocks apart. At the micro level, water collected between soil particles freezes and forms ice 'needles' which expand and displace the surrounding soil. This 'frost heave' uproots poorly anchored plants, making life especially tough for plants growing in exposed positions.

SEDIMENTARY & METAMORPHIC LAYERED ROCKS

Close-up Parallel layers of sedimentary sandstones, mudstones and shales are 'pressure cooked' (metamorphosed) into tougher rocks when they come in contact with molten rock.

At a distance Tilted, folded and uplifted sedimentary and metamorphic rocks form striking ridge and bluff country. That's because weaker layers are eaten away by weathering and erosion, creating an uneven jagged profile.

Where to see layered landforms?

ACT   • Mount Aggie and Boboyan Trig

NSW   • Kosciuszko Road (below Rawsons Pass)
      • On the Main Range Lakes Walk

VIC   • The Bluff
      • Crosscut Saw
      • Mount Feathertop
      • Mount Hotham

PHOTOGRAPH BY DAVID TATNALL ©

The Bluff, Alpine National Park

13

Australian Alps
HABITATS

Going up the mountain? Then get ready for one of nature's most dramatic climatic demonstrations. Nowhere in the world is the influence of temperature, precipitation, soil fertility and shelter so obvious as on a steep mountain slope. This diagram provides a simplified overview of the geographic zones of the Australian Alps, and the habitats that have evolved in response to the changing conditions.

On your drive up, notice how the vegetation changes. The type of plants, the space between them, and their height and shape alter as the altitude increases and the temperature decreases. The ability to cope with colder temperatures, high winds and increased frequency and duration of snowfalls determines which plants survive in the run up to the top of Australia, and which 'fall by the wayside'.

Even the hardiest plants are a shadow of their former selves on the highest ground. The mountain plum-pine, for example, grows to seven metres in cool temperate rainforests. But in the alpine zone it has been reduced to a rock-hugging mat plant.

HABITAT SYMBOL

Look for this symbol next to plants and animals described in this guide. At a glance it tells you in which habitats— and States or Territory—you can expect to see the species. The symbol is colour-coded for the five habitats featured in this guide. If a habitat band is white, the plant or animal in question is unlikely to be found in that habitat.

The Wetlands & Waterways 'swirl' shows the approximate altitudes in which the species might be found. If it is blue from top to bottom, you could expect to find the plant or animal in Wetlands & Waterways from the treeless tops to the foothills. On the other hand, if the swirl is only blue next to the Alpine Heaths & Herbfields habitat, don't expect to see the plant or animal further down the mountain.

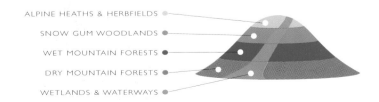

ALPINE HEATHS & HERBFIELDS

SNOW GUM WOODLANDS

WET MOUNTAIN FORESTS

DRY MOUNTAIN FORESTS

WETLANDS & WATERWAYS

ALPINE ZONE	SUBALPINE ZONE	MONTANE	MONTANE
Alpine Heaths & Herbfields	Snow Gum Woodlands	Wet Mountain Forests	Dry Mountain Forests
Above 2000 metres	*1500–2000 metres*	*1000–1500 metres*	*1000–1500 metres*
Above the tree line, a mosaic of low profile grasslands, heaths and herbfields abound. Ground-hugging behaviour is typical and the 'prime real estate'—deep sheltered soils—support short-lived outbursts of seasonal wildflowers in snow-free months.	The higher you climb, the more bent and twisted the trees become. Wracked by blizzards, gales and frost nip, stunted snow gums bow down to a shrubby understorey and a shaggy carpet of snowgrass.	These 'high achievers' are taller than the average timbers. And so they should be, since they've access to year round water, deep rich soils and shelter from drying winds and sunlight.	The mix of eucalypts and shrubs can take the heat from strong sunlight and searing bushfires. There's less water and nutrients to go round and it shows. Trees are shorter and more spread out—more woodland than forest.

snow gum
woodland

feldmark

heaths & herbfields

frost hollow below
tree line due to
cold air drainage

alpine ash
forest

mixed eucalypt
forest

open eucalypt
woodland

WETLANDS & WATERWAYS

Moisture-laden clouds bumping into the Alps are 'milked' for all they're worth. Down comes the rain, hail, sleet and snow. Moss-lined fens, bogs and lakes absorb and hold on to moisture, ensuring year-round supplies.

15

Alpine heaths and herbfields, Kosciuszko National Park

ALPINE HEATHS & HERBFIELDS

Occupying a fraction of the total area of the Australian Alps, treeless alpine areas experience some of the coldest and dampest conditions on the continent, subjecting plant and animal inhabitants to challenging living conditions. Too cold for trees, the high ground supports a patchwork of heaths, grasses and herbs. The amount of exposure to sunlight, degree of shelter, soil fertility, and availability of short term or permanent water supplies influence what grows where. The rolling treeless expanses are regularly exposed to strong winds, driving rain, cracking frosts and intense sunlight.

The year round shattering and weathering of rocks, and relatively slow, chemical breakdown, allows the build up of humus-rich soils on sheltered slopes and valley bottoms. On gentler slopes, massed displays of flowering herbs and shrubs contradict the tough growing conditions. On exposed drier north and west-facing ridges, soils are thinly spread over bare rock, providing a toehold for hardy dwarf feldmark plants. Braving the elements, the latter have little to show for each year's growth.

Where to see Alpine Heaths & Herbfields?

ACT
- The summits of Mounts Franklin and Gingera.

NSW
- Above 1850 metres AND cold air drainage basins below the tree line.
- On the Kosciuszko Road above Charlotte Pass
- From Thredbo Top Station to the Summit

VIC
- Above 1750 metres
- On the Mount Bogong plateau
- On top of Mount Feathertop
- On top of Mount Hotham

ALPINE HEATHS & HERBFIELDS HABITAT

ANIMALS

MAMMALS
27 Short-beaked echidna
29 Common wombat
29 European fox
30 European hare
32 Mountain pygmy-possum
33 Southern bush rat
34 Broad-toothed rat
34 Dusky antechinus
34 Agile antechinus

BIRDS
36 Australian raven
36 Little raven
37 Pied currawong
37 Grey currawong
38 Common starling
38 Wedge-tailed eagle
39 Pacific black duck
39 Brown goshawk
40 Nankeen kestrel
41 Richard's pipit
44 Silvereye

SNAKES
46 Highlands copperhead
47 White-lipped snake

LIZARDS
47 Mountain log skink
48 Alpine water skink
48 Southern water skink
48 Mountain heath dragon

FROGS
49 Southern corroboree frog
49 Common eastern froglet
50 Alpine tree-frog

CRAYFISH
51 Spiny crayfish

INSECTS
51 Mountain grasshopper
52 Mountain spotted grasshopper
52 Alpine thermocolour grasshopper
52 Macleays swallowtail
53 Bogong moth
54 March fly
54 Kosciuszko metallic cockroach
55 Alpine funnelweb
55 Wolf spider

PLANTS

FLOWERING SHRUBS & HERBS
63 Alpine daisy-bush
63 Snow beard-heath
63 Swamp heath
64 Coral heath
64 Alpine baeckea
65 Ovate phebalium
65 Alpine mint-bush
65 Carpet heath
66 Cascade everlasting
67 Alpine everlasting
67 Yarrow
68 Anemone buttercup
68 Silver snow daisy
68 Silky snow daisy
68 Snow daisies
69 Hoary sunray
69 Alpine marsh-marigold
69 Clovers
70 Alpine gentian
70 Glacial eyebright
70 Mauve leek orchid
71 Alpine sundew
71 Mud pratia
71 White purslane
72 Mountain celery
72 Silver ewartia
73 Tall rice flower
73 Candle heath
73 Alpine stackhousia
74 Alpine pepper
74 Alpine orites
74 Alpine bottlebrush
75 Yellow kunzea
75 Alpine wattle
76 Leafy bossiae
77 Alpine shaggy pea
78 Granite buttercup
78 Gunn's alpine buttercup
78 Dandelions
79 Native yam
79 Variable groundsel
79 Ivy-leaf goodenia
80 Alpine podolepis
80 Billy buttons
81 Scaly buttons
81 Button everlasting
81 Golden everlasting

82 Mountain caladenia
82 Alpine rice-flower
83 Grass trigger plant
83 Gunn's willow-herb
84 Royal grevillea
84 Sheep sorrel
84 Bidgee-widgee
85 Mountain plum-pine
86 Alpine hovea
86 Eyebright
86 Showy violet
87 Hebe
87 Sky lily
88 Tasman flax-lily
88 Waxy bluebell
88 Royal bluebell
89 Alpine leek orchid
89 Two-flowered knawel
89 Hard cushion plant
89 Pineapple grass

MOSS & SEDGES
90 Alpine tuft-rush
90 Tufted sedge
90 Sphagnum moss

FERNS
91 Mother shield-fern
91 Alpine water-fern

GRASSES
92 Prickly snow grass
92 Soft snow grass
93 Alpine wallaby grass
93 Ribonny grass

PHOTOGRAPH P GERMAN / NATURE FOCUS

SOUTHERN CORROBOREE FROG

SNOW GUM WOODLANDS

PHOTOGRAPH BY DAVID TATNALL ©

Mount Loch, Alpine National Park

In summer, hardy snow gums cast contorted shadows on a carpet of snowgrass. The heady scents of shrubs and herbs waft through the woodland. A frenzy of birds and insects poke, sip, snap and buzz about their business in the all-too-short growing season before frosts and snow return. But with increasing altitude, the snow gums lose their height and bulk, adopting more stunted postures. Here and there, the woodland is interrupted as 'fingers' of alpine heaths and herbfields dip down below the tree line. Cold air flowing downslope collects, creating frost hollows that make life impossible for snow gum seedlings.

Where to see Snow Gum Woodlands?

ACT • Franklin Road to Mount Ginini

NSW • Sawpit Creek
• Perisher
• Guthega & Thredbo Valleys

VIC • Rocky Creek Dam
• Mount Feathertop slopes

SNOW GUM WOODLAND HABITAT

ANIMALS

MAMMALS

27 Short-beaked echidna
27 Brumby
28 Eastern grey kangaroo
28 Swamp wallaby
28 Red-necked wallaby
29 Feral pig
29 Common wombat
29 European fox
30 European hare
30 Rabbit
31 Mountain brushtail possum
31 Common brushtail possum
31 Common ringtail possum
31 Lesser long-eared bat
32 Eastern pygmy-possum
32 Mountain pygmy-possum
33 Swamp rat
33 Southern bush rat
34 Broad-toothed rat
34 Dusky antechinus
34 Agile antechinus

BIRDS

35 Gang-gang cockatoo
35 Grey shrike-thrush
36 Yellow-tailed black cockatoo
36 Australian raven
36 Little raven
37 Pied currawong
37 Grey currawong
38 Common starling
38 Wedge-tailed eagle
39 Pacific black duck
39 Rufous whistler
39 Brown goshawk
40 Laughing kookaburra
40 Nankeen kestrel
40 Red wattlebird
41 Richard's pipit
41 Fan-tailed cuckoo
41 Grey fantail
42 White-browed scrubwren
42 Brown thornbill

42 White-throated treecreeper
43 Eastern spinebill
43 Yellow-faced honeyeater
43 White-eared honeyeater
44 Silvereye
44 Striated pardalote
44 Spotted pardalote
45 Superb fairy-wren
45 Flame robin
45 Crimson rosella

SNAKES

46 Highlands copperhead
46 Mainland tiger snake
47 White-lipped snake

LIZARDS

47 Mountain log skink
47 Mountain swamp skink
48 Alpine water skink
48 Southern water skink
48 Mountain heath dragon

FROGS

49 Southern corroboree frog
49 Common eastern froglet
50 Alpine tree-frog

CRAYFISH

51 Spiny crayfish

INSECTS

51 Mountain grasshopper
52 Mountain spotted grasshopper
52 Alpine thermocolour grasshopper
52 Macleay's swallowtail
53 Bogong moth
54 March fly
54 Kosciuszko metallic cockroach
55 Palebrown sawfly
55 Alpine funnelweb
55 Wolf spider

PLANTS

TREES

59 Black sally
60 Snow gum
62 Black willow
62 Victorian Christmas bush

FLOWERING SHRUBS & HERBS

63 Dusty daisy-bush
63 Alpine daisy-bush
63 Swamp heath
64 Coral heath
64 Alpine baeckea
64 Woolly tea-tree
65 Ovate phebalium
65 Alpine mint-bush
65 Carpet heath
66 White speedwell
66 Cascade everlasting
67 Common cassinia
67 Alpine everlasting
67 Yarrow
68 Anemone buttercup
68 Silver snow daisy
68 Silky snow daisy
68 Snow daisies
69 Hoary sunray
69 Clover
70 Alpine gentian
70 Glacial eyebright
70 Mauve leek orchid
71 Alpine sundew
71 Mud pratia
71 White purslane
72 Mountain celery
72 Silver ewartia
72 Alpine grevillea
73 Tall rice flower
73 Candle heath
73 Alpine stackhousia
74 Alpine pepper
74 Alpine orites
74 Alpine bottlebrush
75 Yellow kunzea
75 Alpine wattle
75 Mountain hickory wattle
76 Buffalo sallow wattle
76 English broom
76 Leafy bossiae
77 Twiggy mullein

77 Alpine shaggy pea
78 Granite buttercup
78 Gunn's alpine buttercup
78 Dandelions
79 Native yam
79 Variable groundsel
79 Ivy-leaf goodenia
80 Alpine podolepis
80 Clustered everlasting
80 Billy buttons
81 Scaly buttons
81 Button everlasting
81 Golden everlasting
82 Mountain caladenia
82 Alpine boronia
82 Alpine rice-flower
83 Grass trigger plant
83 Gunn's willow-herb
84 Royal grevillea
84 Sheep sorrel
84 Bidgee-widgee
85 Mountain plum-pine
86 Alpine hovea
86 Eyebright
86 Showy violet
87 Sky lily
87 Russell lupin
88 Vipers bugloss
88 Tasman flax-lily
88 Waxy bluebell
88 Royal bluebell
89 Alpine leek orchid
89 Two-flowered knawel
89 Pineapple grass

MOSS & SEDGES

90 Alpine tuft-rush
90 Tufted sedge
90 Sphagnum moss

FERNS

91 Mother shield-fern
91 Alpine water-fern

GRASSES

92 Prickly snow grass
92 Soft snow grass
93 Alpine wallaby grass

WET MOUNTAIN FORESTS

The tallest, straightest trees of the Alps have the best of everything when it comes to growing conditions. The best watered, most sheltered mountainous slopes supply everything a 'reach-for-the-skies' tree might need. The never-ending supply of leaf litter spilling down the slopes enriches the deep organic water-holding soils. And there are no harsh drying winds to ruffle the trees into twisted shapes.

On the sheltered upper slopes, pure stands of fire-sensitive alpine ash (NSW & VIC) and mountain ash (VIC) grow above a sparse understorey of shade-tolerant small trees, shrubs and herbs. Further down the slope, the tall forest opens up a fraction. Peppermints, brown barrel and ribbon gum abound. Because more light reaches the forest floor, the understorey is jam-packed with lush, tall shrubs and herbs.

Where to see
Wet Mountain Forests?

ACT • Along Brindabella, Bendora and Warks roads
• Lyrebird Trail in Tidbinbilla Nature Reserve

NSW • Alpine Way below Leather Barrel Creek
• From Olsen's Lookout

VIC • Falls Creek access road
• Rollasons Falls, Mount Buffalo National Park

PHOTOGRAPH BY DAVID TATNALL ©

Wet mountain forest, Mount Buffalo National Park

WET MOUNTAIN FOREST HABITAT

ANIMALS

MAMMALS
27 Brumby
28 Eastern grey kangaroo
28 Swamp wallaby
28 Red-necked wallaby
29 Feral pig
29 Common wombat
29 European fox
30 Yellow-bellied glider
31 Mountain brushtail possum
31 Common brushtail possum
31 Common ringtail possum
31 Lesser long-eared bat
32 Eastern pygmy-possum
33 Swamp rat
33 Southern bush rat
34 Broad-toothed rat
34 Agile antechinus

BIRDS
35 Wonga pigeon
35 Gang-gang cockatoo
35 Grey shrike-thrush
36 Yellow-tailed black cockatoo
36 Australian raven
36 Little raven
37 Pied currawong
37 Grey currawong
37 Satin bowerbird
38 Wedge-tailed eagle
38 Superb lyrebird
39 Rufous whistler
39 Brown goshawk
40 Laughing kookaburra
40 Red wattlebird
41 Fan-tailed cuckoo
41 Grey fantail
42 White-browed scrubwren
42 Brown thornbill
42 White-throated treecreeper
43 Eastern spinebill
43 Yellow-faced honeyeater

43 White-eared honeyeater
44 Silvereye
44 Striated pardalote
44 Spotted pardalote
45 Superb fairy-wren
45 Flame robin
45 Crimson rosella

SNAKES
46 Highlands copperhead
46 Mainland tiger snake

LIZARDS
47 Mountain swamp skink
48 Southern water skink

FROGS
49 Common eastern froglet

CRAYFISH
51 Spiny crayfish

INSECTS
51 Mountain grasshopper
52 Macleays swallowtail
55 Palebrown sawfly

PLANTS

TREES
57 Mountain ash
57 Alpine ash
58 Brown barrell
58 Mountain gum
59 Ribbon gum
59 Narrow-leaved peppermint
59 Broad-leaved peppermint
59 Black sally
60 Snow gum
61 Blackwood
62 Black willow
62 Silver wattle
62 Victorian Christmas bush

FLOWERING SHRUBS & HERBS
64 Alpine baeckea
64 Woolly tea-tree
66 White speedwell
66 Blackberry
67 Yarrow

68 Clovers
74 Alpine pepper
74 Alpine bottlebrush
75 Mountain hickory wattle
78 Dandelions
83 Mountain correa
85 Mountain plum-pine
85 Round-leaf mint bush
88 Tasman flax-lily
88 Waxy bluebell
89 Two-flowered knawel

MOSS & SEDGES
90 Tufted sedge
90 Sphagnum moss

FERNS
91 Soft tree-fern
91 Mother shield-fern
91 Alpine water-fern

SILVER WATTLE

DRY MOUNTAIN FORESTS

PHOTOGRAPH BY DAVID TATNALL ©

Mount Cobberas, Alpine National Park

Australia's hard-living, hard-leaved plants are well-equipped to cope with life on the dry side. You can't miss them on the mountain ridges and foothills that make up the bulk of the Australian Alps. Periodic bushfires, droughts, low altitude snowfalls and frosts are to be expected. Extensive open forests of mixed eucalypts, and other medium height trees clothe exposed north and west-facing slopes, thriving on sun-baked soils in high evaporation zones. Water conservation strategies are essential on drier rainshadow slopes as clouds have often dropped their load by the time they pass overhead. As the trees spread out, there's less organic matter to go round, and it breaks down quickly. Key dry forest trees include the broad-leaved peppermint, candlebark and the fire-resistant red stringybark. On drier ridges, cypress pines prevail over an understorey of shrubs and grasses.

Where to see Dry Mountain Forests?

ACT
- Mount Clear campground
- Lower reaches of Cotter River valley
- Warmer slopes en route to Booroomba Rocks

NSW
- Between Jindabyne & Waste Point

VIC
- On the lower reaches of the drive up to Falls Creek
- On the lower reaches of the drive up to Mount Hotham

DRY MOUNTAIN FOREST HABITAT

ANIMALS

MAMMALS

27 Short-beaked echidna
27 Brumby
28 Eastern grey kangaroo
28 Swamp wallaby
28 Red-necked wallaby
29 Feral pig
29 Common wombat
29 European fox
30 European hare
30 Rabbit
30 Yellow-bellied glider
31 Mountain brushtail possum
31 Common brushtail possum
31 Common ringtail possum
31 Lesser long-eared bat
32 Eastern pygmy-possum
33 Swamp rat
33 Southern bush rat
34 Broad-toothed rat
34 Agile antechinus

BIRDS

35 Gang-gang cockatoo
35 Grey shrike-thrush
36 Yellow-tailed black cockatoo
36 Australian raven
36 Little raven
37 Pied currawong
37 Grey currawong
38 Common starling
38 Wedge-tailed eagle
38 Superb lyrebird
39 Pacific black duck
39 Rufous whistler
39 Brown goshawk
40 Laughing kookaburra
40 Nankeen kestrel
40 Red wattlebird
41 Fan-tailed cuckoo
41 Grey fantail
42 White-browed scrubwren
42 Brown thornbill
42 White-throated treecreeper
43 Eastern spinebill

43 Yellow-faced honeyeater
43 White-eared honeyeater
44 Silvereye
44 Striated pardalote
44 Spotted pardalote
45 Superb fairy-wren
45 Flame robin
45 Crimson rosella

SNAKES

46 Highlands copperhead
46 Red-bellied black snake
46 Mainland tiger snake
47 White-lipped snake

LIZARDS

47 Mountain log skink
48 Mountain heath dragon

INSECTS

51 Mountain grasshopper
52 Macleays swallowtail
54 March fly
55 Palebrown sawfly

PLANTS

TREES

58 Candlebark
58 Mountain gum
59 Ribbon gum
59 Narrow-leaved peppermint
59 Broad-leaved peppermint
60 Snow gum
61 Radiata pine
61 Black cypress
62 Black willow
62 Silver wattle
62 Victorian Christmas bush

FLOWERING SHRUBS & HERBS

63 Dusty daisy-bush
64 Woolly tea-tree
66 Blackberry
67 Common cassinia
67 Yarrow
69 Clover
75 Yellow kunzea

75 Mountain hickory wattle
76 English broom
76 Leafy bossiae
77 Twiggy mullein
77 St Johns wort
77 Alpine shaggy pea
78 Dandelions
79 Native yam
80 Alpine podolepis
82 Alpine boronia
83 Grass trigger Plant
83 Mountain correa
84 Bidgee-widgee
85 Scotch thistle
87 Russell lupin
88 Vipers bugloss
88 Tasman flax-lily
89 Two-flowered knawel

GRASSES

93 Kangaroo grass

PHOTOGRAPH D WATTS / NATURE FOCUS

SHORT-BEAKED ECHIDNA

Lake Albina, Kosciuszko National Park

WETLANDS & WATERWAYS

Squish, squelsh, splash! Anyone who's found their way blocked by a roaring, swollen spring-melt river has an inkling of the enormous volume of water trapped in the Alps as snow and ice during winter. The fens, spongy bogs, lakes and headwaters of the highest country play a crucial role in storing rainwater, sleet and snowmelt, preventing too-rapid runoff and keeping the mountains green. Sad to say, mountain wetlands have been severely damaged by hard-hooved livestock and annual burning off. Ironically, most of the conservation reserves making up the Australian Alps were set aside primarily to protect their catchment values. Indeed their ability to generate and trap precipitation brought them to the attention of the wider community. Hydro-electric power generating schemes were implemented in the NSW and Victorian alps to harness their 'excess' waters.

Where to see Wetlands & Waterways?

ACT
- Cotter River, below Bendora and Corin Dams
- Nursery Swamp

NSW
- The Lakes Walk via Charlotte Pass
- The Summit Walk from Thredbo Top Station
- Yarrangobilly Caves

VIC
- Watchbed Creek above Falls Creek
- Lower Snowy River
- Lake Catani, Mount Buffalo National Park

WETLANDS & WATERWAYS HABITAT

ANIMALS

MAMMALS
27 Platypus
33 Water rat
33 Swamp rat

BIRDS
39 Pacific black duck

SNAKES
46 Red-bellied black snake

LIZARDS
48 Alpine water skink
48 Southern water skink

FROGS
49 Southern corroboree frog
49 Common eastern froglet
50 Alpine tree-frog

FISH
50 Brown trout
50 Rainbow trout
51 Mountain galaxias

CRAYFISH
51 Spiny crayfish

PLANTS

TREES
62 Black willow

FLOWERING SHRUBS & HERBS
64 Coral heath
64 Alpine baeckea
64 Woolly tea-tree
69 Alpine marsh-marigold
71 Alpine sundew
71 White purslane
73 Candle heath
74 Alpine bottlebrush

MOSS & SEDGES
90 Alpine tuft-rush
90 Tufted sedge
90 Sphagnum moss

FERNS
91 Alpine water-fern

PHOTOGRAPH D WATTS / NATURE IOCUS

PLATYPUS

Introduction to Australian Alps
ANIMALS

What type of animals are found in the Australian Alps? Some high-living animals, such as kangaroos, possums, wombats, platypus, wattlebirds and currawongs, thrive in a range of habitats from the mountains to the sea. But a handful are found nowhere else in Australia, or the world. Because of the extreme conditions, some of the wildlife are part-timers. The arrival of winter separates the stayers from summer 'blow-ins'. If food shortages are likely, mobile species amble, hop or fly to lower altitudes or warmer northerly climates.

Who goes? In alpine and subalpine zones, insect-eating animals are more likely to leave the mountains because their insect food supply overwinters in the snow-covered soil as eggs or caterpillars.

Who stays? As winter looms, the availability of food controls which animals can afford to stay. Birds that feed on gum nuts and seeds have whole mountainsides of trees and shrubs to choose from, and less need to leave the mountains. While some mammals move down the mountain to more sheltered tracts others, including the wombat and fox, are equipped to burrow through the snow for buried plant matter. For smaller less mobile mammals, staying put is the only option once a snowy blanket has been cast over the mountains. Strange as it sounds, a 20 centimetre snow cover is thick enough to insulate small mammals from the worst of the weather. Out of the wind and in the dark, some huddle together for warmth, or live off fat reserves built up during the warmer months. A handful of small mammals are able to reduce their energy needs by sleeping for days at a time, while mountain pygmy-possums hibernate for much of the winter. As for reptiles, some species hole up over winter, nurturing their unborn young. Others lay eggs in autumn and trust they will survive the winter deep freeze.

WHEN TO SEE?

Your chances of seeing a particular animal are just that—chancy. Catching sight of an animal, however common, depends on your being in the right place at the right time to witness its coming and going. Overcast weather might increase your chances in summer, prompting dusk-to-dawners to become active earlier than usual. Wet, windy or extra cold weather might put off all but the hungriest warm-blooded animals, especially in exposed locations. This guide gives you an idea of when animals in the Australian Alps are most likely to be seen. So count yourself lucky if you come across a species outside our suggested timezones.

 indicates that an animal is mainly day-active —out and about during the day.

 indicates that an animal is mainly night-active —out and about from dusk until dawn.

ACTIVE ALL YEAR indicates that the animal may be seen throughout the year, especially at lower altitudes where the climate is milder.

SPRING or SUMMER indicates that the animal is either a spring or summer visitor to the Alps, OR becomes inactive over winter, and hence invisible.

SHORT-BEAKED ECHIDNA
Tachyglossus aculeatus

 ACTIVE SUMMER

What's the best defence for snowbound echidnas? Most drop their body temperature and hibernate in a hollow log or burrow. *Why hibernate?* If your diet is over 90% ants—and ants survive the winter as eggs —a deep sleep is a sensible survival strategy. When echidnas 'come to' around mid-winter, it's possible they mate beneath the snow, regardless of

HABITAT
ACT • NSW • VIC

gales and blizzards raging overhead. The next generation are well on the way by the time the snow melts.
Droppings Echidnas are responsible for dig marks around ant nests. They also mass produce distinctive sparkling cyclindrical droppings chockful of—you guessed it—*ants!*

PLATYPUS
Ornithorhynchus anatinus

 ACTIVE ALL YEAR

Icy dips in snow fed streams are not a problem for these egg-laying mammals. *How do platypuses manage to keep their body temperature a snug 32˚C during lengthy dips in 0˚C pools?* Their thick fur coat acts as a water resistant 'wet suit', even in subalpine pools. And the platypus's burrow entrances are designed to squeeze out excess water on entry.

A rat or plat? Picking the difference between a

HABITAT
ACT • NSW • VIC

platypus and a water rat is difficult in poor light. Look for the water rat's prominent ears and the platypus's smoother swimming style and tell-tale bow wave.

HABITAT
ACT • NSW • VIC

BRUMBY
Equus caballus

F E R A L species

 ACTIVE ALL YEAR

It's easy to get sentimental over the 'wild bush horses' immortalised in Banjo Paterson's 'Man From Snowy River' and Elynne Mitchell's 'Silver Brumby' stories. But these descendants of runaway stock are hard on the high country. Because its weight is borne by small hooves, the feral horse is capable of inflicting heavy damage on sensitive subalpine vegetation. Grazing pressure, and weeds spread in brumby droppings add to the damage.

EASTERN GREY KANGAROO
Macropus giganteus

☾ ACTIVE ALL YEAR

HABITAT
ACT • NSW • VIC

PHOTOGRAPH D WATTS / NATURE IOCUS

Immortalised in the 'Skippy' TV program, the eastern grey kangaroo is the largest macropod you'll see in the snow country. It's also the most sociable, resting and feeding as a family. But its 'safety in numbers' policy doesn't apply to roadside grazing. Keep a sharp lookout if you're driving through the Australian Alps, especially from dusk till dawn. Roos are blinded by headlights.

P.S. If you're camping, don't offer over-friendly roos human 'junk food', bread included. They're much better off sticking to snowgrass.

PHOTOGRAPH D WATTS / NATURE IOCUS

SWAMP WALLABY
Wallabia bicolor

☾ ACTIVE ALL YEAR

• brown to black-flecked back fur, yellow to orange chest

HABITAT
ACT • NSW • VIC

A loner by nature, this small wallaby has the perfect camouflage for forest dwelling—a mottled fur coat the colour of stagnant water. With head held low and in line with its tail, the 'swampy' bullets through thick forest understorey. While it's partial to snowgrasses and shrubs, special cutting teeth allow this browser to tackle tougher foods, including bracken fern and tree seedlings.

RED-NECKED WALLABY
Macropus rufogriseus

☾ ACTIVE ALL YEAR

• red neck fur and rump

HABITAT
ACT • NSW • VIC

PHOTOGRAPH D WATTS / NATURE IOCUS

If it's alone, makes a hop for cover, and has a grey to reddish fur coat, you've probably spotted a red-necked wallaby. Wet or overcast conditions are the best time to see a red-neck by day. That's when they're most likely to throw caution to the wind and leave dense forest thickets to graze in snow gum woodlands. On the few occasions they gang up for a nightly feed, they split up if disturbed—*each to its own*.

FERAL PIG
Sus scrofa

HABITAT

ACT • NSW • VIC

🌙 ACTIVE SUMMER

Cute pets? *Not for long!* Outgrowing their 'babe' days, too many pigs are breeding freely, swelling the ranks of Australia's most troublesome agricultural escapee. In the snow-free months, pigrooting below the tree line causes maximum damage in the minimum time. Feral pigs keep their skin supple by wallowing in damp areas, including fragile sphagnum bogs. Woe betide snowgrasses and other plants that stand in the way of a pig and its dinner of plant roots and bulbs. Worse still, there's plenty more where they came from, with sows producing *up to 14 'babes' a year!*

COMMON WOMBAT
Vombatus ursinus

🌙 ACTIVE ALL YEAR

HABITAT

ACT • NSW • VIC

From their woodland nesting burrows, wombats venture out in all weathers to eat leaves, and unearth roots and fungi. While a bulky build and thick fur coat ward off the cold, wombats flounder in deep soft snow, and tend to stick to regular pathways. They also feed along roadsides. *That's why it pays to slow down and stay alert while night driving in the Australian Alps!*

PHOTOGRAPH D WATTS / NATURE fOCUS

EUROPEAN FOX
Vulpes vulpes

☀ 🌙 ACTIVE ALL YEAR

Sad but true, the mammal you're most likely to spot on the treeless tops is the European red fox. *How come?* They're big, plentiful and hunt in broad daylight. Each fox family presides over some 10 square kilometres of alpine country. Unfortunately their 'country seat' is most likely to be located in rock piles, the natural refuge of the mountain pygmy-possum and other small mammals. That's a bit too *close for comfort*, especially when the fox uses sniffer dog skills to locate warm-blooded 'snack food' sheltering under the snow, including broad-toothed rats.

INTRODUCED species

HABITAT

ACT • NSW • VIC

EUROPEAN HARE
Lepus europaeus

🌙 ACTIVE ALL YEAR

It's easy to see why the European hare has made itself at home in the highest alpine tracts. Superb digging skills extend to snow as well as soil. Food's no problem either. Even in winter, there's an unlimited supply of frozen poa (snowgrass). Hares compete with native wildlife on their own patch, and at higher altitudes scratch out native shrubs, herbs and grasses.

HABITAT

ACT • NSW • VIC

P.S. Don't quench your thirst on orange snow. *Chances are a hare's been there!*

RABBIT
Orcytolagus cuniculus

🌙 ACTIVE ALL YEAR

HABITAT

ACT • NSW • VIC

On lower plains where the snow cover is patchy, rabbits come into their own. S*now bunnies?* Not often! In fact they neither warm to the cold nor to snowgrass. *Most likely hang-outs?* Sown pastures, along roadsides and around ski resorts. Frankly we hope you *don't* see any.

YELLOW-BELLIED GLIDER
Petaurus australis

🌙 ACTIVE ALL YEAR

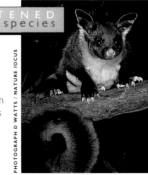

A 100 metres *in a single glide?* Turns 90° corners *mid air?* Gliding skills aside, the highly vocal yellow-bellied glider lives in communes of females and youngsters ruled by a dominant male. W*here?* They nest in rotted out tree hollows that only form in tall, aged eucalypts. The loss of 'old growth' forest giants to logging or wildfires evicts individual gliders and entire communities.

Tree's 'milk'? Generation after generation of these gliders suck the sugary energy-rich sap of ribbon (manna) gums, leaving tell-tale scars on the bark.

HABITAT

ACT • NSW • VIC

Give away call? If you're walking through tall forests at night and hear a noise like a *pig squealing,* followed by a cappuccino machine *gurgle,* congratulations! You're in yellow-bellied glider territory.

MOUNTAIN BRUSHTAIL POSSUM
Trichosurus caninus

🌙 ACTIVE ALL YEAR

You're unlikely to see the 'bobuck' possum unless camping or

HABITAT

ACT • NSW • VIC

spotlighting. Its agile limbs come in handy when lifting the lids on garbage bins. *A word of warning.* Lock up your food and don't encourage wild animals! Over-bold bobucks are better off eating foliage, fruits, fungi, lichen and bark. *Yummo!*

COMMON BRUSHTAIL POSSUM
Trichosurus vulpecula

🌙 ACTIVE ALL YEAR

HABITAT

ACT • NSW • VIC

Below the winter snowline, you are more likely to spot the look-alike common brushtail possum. It's widespread throughout Australian open forests and woodlands.

COMMON RINGTAIL POSSUM
Pseudocheirus peregrinus

🌙 ACTIVE ALL YEAR

Using its grasping tail as a fifth 'limb', the ringtail is an agile climber

HABITAT

ACT • NSW • VIC

and leaper, and rarely descends to the woodland floor, particularly when it's snow-covered. *Why bother?* Its food supply—gum leaves, shoots and flowers—is plentiful above ground. It nests in a football-sized 'drey' of twigs, bark, ferns and grass.

LESSER LONG-EARED BAT
Nyctophilus geoffroyi

🌙 ACTIVE SUMMER

HABITAT

ACT • NSW • VIC

What was that? If it's a mild summer evening and you're in a woodland clearing or by a river, that thing flitting past might be a bat. The lesser long-eared is one of six bats recorded above 1400 metres in the Alps. *Lesser?* It's only 6–8 gms. The *largest*, the white-striped mastiff bat (around 35 gms), is lured into the alpine zone by the summer 'smorgasbord' of bogong moths.

mammals

31

PHOTOGRAPH G LITTLE / NATURE FOCUS

EASTERN PYGMY-POSSUM
Cercatetus nanus

🌙 ACTIVE SUMMER

HABITAT

ACT • NSW • VIC

The eastern pygmy-possum takes *time out* if the going gets tough, or food supply drops suddenly. *How?* It can lapse into torpor for 2–3 days at a time. *What does it eat?* A balanced diet of nectar, pollen, fruit and insects. *Where does it live?* While it's more at home in the lower part of the subalpine zone, it has been recorded at the tree line (1800 metres) in the ACT.

- fawn back & pale to white underside
- 9 cm long body and tail

MOUNTAIN PYGMY-POSSUM
Burramys parvus

🌙 ACTIVE SUMMER

HABITAT

NSW • VIC

- 11 cm long body
- 14 cm curled tail

Less than 10 square kilometres of Australia's highest ground is potential habitat for this mouse-sized pygmy-possum. During summer there's no shortage of food around its rocky retreat, including grasshoppers, beetles and spiders. Add to that the fruit of the mountain plum-pine and mountain beard heath. And don't forget the hordes of bogong moths which share its hideout and make up over 30% of its diet. The pygmy-possum relies on summer feasting to build up enough fat reserves to last the winter with minimal food intake.

How does it pass the time? Insulated under a snow 'blanket', it survives *The Big Chill* in a state of Deep Sleep (hibernation) for up to seven months of the year, probably inside a grassy nest tucked under boulders. Perhaps that's why it wasn't 'discovered' until 1966. Prior to that scientists assumed that the pygmy-possum they knew as a fossil was *extinct!*

What's threatening this pygmy-possum?
Threat Number 1 For most of its existence, it's had few natural enemies. But the spread this century of foxes and feral cats has placed it on

PHOTOGRAPH G A HOYE / NATURE FOCUS

THREATENED species

a *guerilla war* footing. Put a paw wrong and the pygmy-possum is likely to be 'snaffled'.

Threat Number 2 Roads, ski trails and other developments cut through the animal's territory, separating potential mates. Slope grooming and snowmaking may wake pygmy-possums during the coldest months, draining limited energy reserves and stamina.

Threat Number 3 Oddly enough, the biggest challenge for this secretive creature could be *The Big Unchill* predicted to result from global warming. *What's the problem?* Less snow means a thinner cover, which would expose pygmy-possums to the extremes of autumn frosts and gales. Adjusting to thinner snows could be like sleeping under a *sheet* when used to a *doona!*

WATER RAT
Hydromys chrysogaster

☀ ☽ ACTIVE ALL YEAR

- 30 cm head-body length
- white-tipped 27 cm long tail
- gold to orange underfur

HABITAT

ACT • NSW • VIC

Partially webbed feet and waterproof fur help equip the *biggest rat* in the Australian Alps for an aquatic life. *Where and when to see it?* In and around waterways late in the day. Nesting in streambank burrows, it patrols the waterways for fish, aquatic insect larvae, freshwater crayfish and even water skinks. Unlike the platypus (which it's sometimes mistaken for), the water rat is a *wimp* when it comes to cold water, so you're more likely to see it below the subalpine zone.

SWAMP RAT
Rattus lutreolus

☀ ☽ ACTIVE ALL YEAR

- 164 mm average head-body length, 113 mm tail length
- grey-brown above, paler below

HABITAT

NSW • VIC

Swamps? This rat is equally at home in sedges, heaths and grasses, wet or dry. While it takes the plunge to get from A to B, the swamp rat lacks the swimming skills of the water rat. *Why is it one of the few native rats that's day-active?* Because it eats its way through the undergrowth, chomping out 'runways', it can go about its business by day undetected. Therein lies a problem. If the vegetation is removed through clearing or burning, the rat's *cover* is blown and the population plummets.

SOUTHERN BUSH RAT
Rattus fuscipes

☽ ACTIVE ALL YEAR

HABITAT

ACT • NSW • VIC

This is the rat most likely to disturb campers bunking down in high country huts—one of the *many good reasons to* BYO tent! It's naturally at home along subalpine creek banks and bogs. Come winter, some bush rats vacate metre-long burrows for the higher alpine herbfields. That's because snow offers better insulation than foliage, keeping temperatures around the zero degree mark. It also hides them from foxes. *What do bush rats eat to keep up energy?* Insects, including snap-frozen 'corpses' washed downstream in spring, and fruit, fungi, flowers, leaves and seeds.

33

mammals

BROAD-TOOTHED RAT
Mastacomys fuscus

🌙 ACTIVE ALL YEAR

- •160 mm head body length
- •average tail 110 mm long

The broad-toothed rat is a big eater, consuming around 50–70% of its body weight each day—mainly grasses and sedges. But much of what goes in comes out

HABITAT

ACT • NSW • VIC

the other end in the form of 200–400 yellowish droppings *per day*, some of which are recycled (*re-eaten!*). Slow on its feet, this podgy rat sports an impressively fluffy fur coat. Greenish tips—due to algal growth—are a legacy of this rat's liking for damp habitats!

P.S. *The broad-toothed rat keeps active throughout winter beneath the snow.*

DUSKY ANTECHINUS
Antechinus swainsonii

HABITAT

ACT • NSW • VIC

🌙 ACTIVE ALL YEAR

Equally at home in coastal areas, in the Australian Alps the dusky antechinus mainly lives in shrubby woodlands and heaths, above the 1600 metre mark (*including on top of Mount Kosciuszko!*). The dark-furred, pointy-nosed antechinus seeks cover under shrubs and bushes, favouring damper sites. It burrows under rocks or nests in tree hollows. While grassy areas may be 'no go' zones in summer, *come winter*, the added blanket of snow reduces the risk of being spotted by predators. *What does it eat?* Grasshoppers, moths, beetles, bugs, flies, cockroaches, worms, spiders and lizards fall prey to its long foreclaws and pincer teeth.

AGILE ANTECHINUS
Antechinus agilis

🌙 ACTIVE ALL YEAR

HABITAT

ACT • NSW • VIC

What's the difference between the dusky and agile antechinus? While they share a similar diet, the agile antechinus has a smaller build, smaller claws and a lighter colour overall. The agile antechinus ventures above the tree line but is found in greater numbers in the subalpine zone, favouring rock-strewn woodlands. Strictly nocturnal, this restless marsupial practises communal nesting, an energy-conserving strategy in colder climates.

WONGA PIGEON
Leucosarcia melanoleuca

 ACTIVE ALL YEAR

'*Coo coo. Wonk-a?*' A capable walker, the solitary wonga pigeon feeds on fallen fruits and seeds on forest floors. A wary bird, it makes a quick getaway if disturbed, with a *noisy clap* of the wings. What a shame so few people witness the display the male puts on to impress potential mates. Apparently the female finds the synchronised head swinging, and lifting of tail and wings quite mesmerising. Before long, they're a '*pigeon pair*'.

HABITAT
ACT • NSW • VIC

GANG-GANG COCKATOO
Callocephalon fimbriatum

 ACTIVE ALL YEAR

- drawn out 'rusty door' screech
- slow, laboured flight

HABITAT
ACT • NSW • VIC

'*Cre-ak! Cre-ak!*' That's no squeaky door, it's a gang-gang! Gangs of these noisy cockatoos brave the winter snows, methodically stripping snow gums of their nuts, tree by tree. You're most likely to detect them cracking gumnut seeds, growling all the while and littering the ground—and you—with discarded leaves, nuts and berries. **P.S.** Grey gang-gangs are either *juveniles* or *females*. The jaffa orange crests are unique to the males.

GREY SHRIKE-THRUSH
Colluricincla harmonica

 ACTIVE ALL YEAR

HABITAT
ACT • NSW • VIC

Famous for its rhythmic song, the shrike-thrush stays put in the woodland year round. In summer, it dines out on insects, small lizards, mammals and even birds. Come winter, it's lifting off peeling strips of snow gum bark in search of lurking insects. How does that song go? '*Purr-purr-queee-yule, purr-purr-he-whew-it! Pip-pip-pip-pip-ho-eeee!*'

YELLOW-TAILED BLACK COCKATOO
Calyptorhynchus funereus

☀ ACTIVE ALL YEAR

HABITAT

ACT • NSW • VIC

Talk about loud! Whether they're de-barking a tree, or winging over the mountains with their 'wee-ya' squawks, these cockatoos make their presence *heard*! Detecting hidden wood-boring grubs, they bite out chunks of tree to uncover their prey, perching on bark strips while they chip, chip away with powerful beaks.

• noisy eaters
• slow wing beats

PHOTOGRAPH R DRUMMOND / NATURE IOCUS

AUSTRALIAN RAVEN
Corvus coronoides

☀ ACTIVE ALL YEAR

HABITAT

ACT • NSW • VIC

From the scruffy throat of the Australian raven comes a mournful 'aah aah aaaa—h', with the last 'aaah' dropping off. Look for it in grasslands and foothills, probing tussocks for insects, seeds and sometimes carrion.

PHOTOGRAPH T & P GARDNER / NATURE IOCUS

LITTLE RAVEN
Corvus mellori

☀ ACTIVE ALL YEAR

HABITAT

ACT • NSW • VIC

'Ark, ark ark'. Regularly heard cawing from rocky outcrops, the little raven is much commoner in the Alps than the larger Australian raven. That's partly because the latter tends to nest in tall trees lower down the mountain, while the sleeker little raven sets up house in snow gum woodlands.

Why flap several kilometres to the treeless tops and back? In two words, bogong moths—millions of them. Once the surviving moths depart, grasshoppers and casemoths are in the raven's sights.

PHOTOGRAPH T & P GARDNER / NATURE IOCUS

PHOTOGRAPH G LITTLE / NATURE FOCUS

PIED CURRAWONG
Strepera graculina

☀ ACTIVE ALL YEAR

- magnificent songster
- yellow-eyed
- white patch on primary wing feathers

HABITAT

ACT • NSW • VIC

This aggressive currawong leaves no stick unturned or loose flap of bark unprobed as it patrols the woodlands. Stick insects—especially the plump egg-filled females—have good reason to be nervous, as do young birds. Large gangs of currawongs gather to feast on bogong moths around rocky outcrops. Some fly out when winter approaches, drawn to the bright lights *and overflowing garbage bins* of the big cities.

GREY CURRAWONG
Strepera versicolor

☀ ACTIVE ALL YEAR

HABITAT

ACT • NSW • VIC

Less gregarious, less widespread and slightly larger than its pied 'cousin', this browner-grey currawong has a plainer gong-like call, and feeds mainly on insects.

PHOTOGRAPH R DRUMMOND / NATURE FOCUS

PHOTOGRAPH T & P GARDNER / NATURE FOCUS

SATIN BOWERBIRD
Ptilonorhynchus violaceus

☀ ACTIVE ALL YEAR

HABITAT

ACT • NSW • VIC

Every male bower bird needs a bower, and it's not just for solitude. *More like an elaborate lure.* On the strength of his blue-bedecked 'boudoir', the blue-black male attracts the green-feathered females and persuades, or bullies, one into mating. Perhaps the array of blue knick-knacks provides a measure of his collecting skills, be they flowers, berries, feathers, pegs or buttons.

COMMON STARLING
Sturnus vulgaris

 ACTIVE SUMMER

This European import has an unfair advantage over native birds. Producing four chicks at a time, it rears *two batches* for each native bird's one. On top of that, it ruthlessly competes for nest holes and

HABITAT

ACT • NSW • VIC

sites. When eviction doesn't work, it slaps up a nest over the top of a native bird's. *Revenge is sweet* for brown falcons and brown goshawks which plunder flocks of these noisy insect-eating starlings.

WEDGE-TAILED EAGLE
Aquila audax

 ACTIVE SUMMER

HABITAT

ACT • NSW • VIC

For hundreds of thousands years before the invention of hang gliders, 'wedgies' soared up to 2000 metres above the Alps on their 2.5 metre wingspans. *What's on the menu for Australia's largest bird of prey?* Carrion, road kills and dead or ailing sheep and lambs. As for live prey, rabbits make up the bulk of the eagle's catch, followed by native reptiles, young wallabies and roos, and cockatoos.

PHOTOGRAPH D WATTS / NATURE fOCUS

SUPERB LYREBIRD
Menura novaehollandiae

 ACTIVE ALL YEAR

To attract potential mates, the male lyrebird collects distinctive songs and sound effects from its neighbours. Any female drawn to its 'samplings' is treated to the dance of the lyre tail feathers. But it's a short-lived coupling. All that the female can

HABITAT

ACT • NSW • VIC

expect from the male is a set of genes. There's no chance that he will stick around and construct a nest, *let alone help rear the offspring*!

PHOTOGRAPH D WATTS / NATURE fOCUS

PACIFIC BLACK DUCK
Anas superciliosa

☀ ACTIVE SUMMER

HABITAT
ACT • NSW • VIC

High country haven? It certainly is for the black ducks that wing in for the summer. The majority of alpine lakes and headwaters have escaped agricultural or drainage alterations. Nor are they ringed by hunters keen to bring down Australia's most popular game bird. *What does the black duck eat*? They strip seeds from sedges and other water plants, with crayfish and insects making up the other 25% of the diet.
In the grassy foothills and tablelands, look out for the yellow-eyed Australian wood duck which returns in large numbers each year to feed on grasses and camp by waterways.

RUFOUS WHISTLER
Pachycephala rufiventris

 ☀ ACTIVE SUMMER

HABITAT
ACT • NSW • VIC

If you're walking through open woodlands, keep an ear out for the rufous whistler's boisterous musical *'eee-chong'* and *'joey-joey-joey'*. Often seen in pairs, the whistler wings in for the summer, giving snow gums and other trees the once, twice and three times over for lurking insects.

BROWN GOSHAWK
Accipiter fasciatus

 ☀ ACTIVE SUMMER

This slow-flying 'stealth machine' hugs the tree tops till it spots a prey, chasing small birds through the snow gums, including starlings and crimson rosellas. You could possibly confuse it with the similar sized, less commonly seen brown falcon.

HABITAT
ACT • NSW • VIC

How to tell the difference? Only the goshawk has yellow eyes, banded legs and chest, and 'finger-tipped' wings.

PHOTOGRAPH D WHITFORD / NATURE IOCUS

PHOTOGRAPH F PARK / A.N.T. PHOTO LIBRARY

PHOTOGRAPH T A WAITE / NATURE IOCUS

LAUGHING KOOKABURRA

Dacelo novaeguineae

 ACTIVE ALL YEAR

HABITAT

ACT • NSW • VIC

Having staked out a woodland territory, kookaburras hold onto it for up to 20 years, relying on laughter *as the best defence!* Their raucous chorus is a sounding of *who's who* and *where* in an extended family group, a kind of boundary marking and asserting of rights.

A slow breeder, this largest of kingfishers is prone to population crashes if its habitat is destroyed or altered. For starters, kookaburras can't get by without their *nesting hollows.*

PHOTOGRAPH B L GRAINGER / NATURE FOCUS

NANKEEN KESTREL

Falco cenchroides

 ACTIVE SUMMER

HABITAT

ACT • NSW • VIC

The Australian Alps are a land of milk and honey (grasshoppers and bogong moths more likely) for this energetic kestrel. That's why they *hover* above grasslands and rocky outcrops in summer, swooping on anything that moves. The kestrel's tastes also run to casemoth grubs which eat out patches of snowgrass if not kept in check.

PHOTOGRAPH D WATTS / NATURE FOCUS

PHOTOGRAPH T HOWARD / NATURE FOCUS

RED WATTLEBIRD

Anthochaera carunculata

ACTIVE SPRING – SUMMER

• *raucous call*

HABITAT

ACT • NSW • VIC

Like many woodland honeyeaters, the red wattlebird makes a 'birdline' for royal grevillea flowers when it arrives in spring. Don't be surprised if it looks familiar. In the warmer months, wattlebirds dine out on insects and spiders in many *suburban gardens.*

RICHARD'S PIPIT
Anthus novaeseelandiae

☀ ACTIVE SPRING – SUMMER

HABITAT
ACT • NSW • VIC

The ball of feathers that explodes out of treeless heaths and grasses is probably Richard's pipit —*especially if it's trilling its head off.* The pipit's fetching song flight is designed to impress female mates. Could its 'P*sippitt*' call also be a ploy to lure big-footed humans away from its ground level nest?

FAN-TAILED CUCKOO
Cacomantis flabelliformis

☀ ACTIVE SPRING

HABITAT
ACT • NSW • VIC

'Takeover merchants' by nature, cuckoos are nest invaders (or brood parasites), with brown thornbills the most likely losers in snow gum woodlands. Despite their antisocial habit of laying eggs in another bird's nest, the mournful-sounding cuckoos do a good job of keeping caterpillars in check. This saves gum leaves from undue *munching.*

GREY FANTAIL
Rhipidura fuliginosa

☀ ACTIVE SPRING – SUMMER

This 'mad fan' is non-stop action. Arriving in spring, it darts about the woodlands, taking insects on the wing. If they're in hiding, the grey fantail flits through the foliage. Dropping its wings, it fans its tail to *flush out* insects sheltering under bark and leaves.

HABITAT
ACT • NSW • VIC

41

WHITE-BROWED SCRUBWREN
Sericornis frontalis

☀ ACTIVE ALL YEAR

For little birds bunkering down under the snow, keeping up body heat is vital, especially when food is short. *How do they cope?* Fluffing out their feather 'duvets' helps trap warm air.

HABITAT

ACT • NSW • VIC

Tucking heads under shoulders also reduces heat loss. And then there's shivering. *Did you know that shivering is the muscles' way of warming you up?* The downside is that it uses up valuable energy. A*nd the last resort?* Slowing down body metabolism.

PHOTOGRAPH T & P GARDNER / NATURE fOCUS

PHOTOGRAPH M R WILLIS / NATURE fOCUS

BROWN THORNBILL
Acanthiza pusilla

☀ ACTIVE ALL YEAR

- short warble
- clever mimic

HABITAT

ACT • NSW • VIC

Many thornbills stay put for the winter. A blanket of snow insulates their snug domed nests constructed behind fallen logs or in the undergrowth. An insect eater, the thornbill forages year round on snow gum trunks and foliage, and shrubs.

WHITE-THROATED TREECREEPER
Cormobates leucophaeus

☀ ACTIVE ALL YEAR

This stay-put bird might be the only living thing heard when ski-touring through snow gum groves. *How does it cope with winter?*

HABITAT

ACT • NSW • VIC

PHOTOGRAPH F PARK / A.N.T. PHOTO LIBRARY

Snow gum hollows provide year round, weatherproof shelter for the bird's bark, fur and feather-lined nest. In search of energy food, tree creepers spiral around trunks and branches. It's only a matter of time before insects in hiding under loose bark or in fissures *are sprung!*

EASTERN SPINEBILL
Acanthorhynchus tenuirostris

 ACTIVE SPRING

HABITAT
ACT • NSW • VIC

It's no coincidence that this little spinebill throngs woodlands and heaths from late August till the end of December. That's when the royal grevillea and other nectar-rich plants are in flower. Its elongated spine bill is *a perfect match* for tubular flowers, reaching right to the very end. *Best place to see?* Out-of-the-wind subalpine valleys.

YELLOW-FACED HONEYEATER
Lichenostomus chrysops

 ACTIVE SPRING – SUMMER

HABITAT
ACT • NSW • VIC

Quick off the mark, flocks of yellow-faced honeyeaters zero in on nectar-rich royal grevillea flowers each spring. They also fill up on sugary lerps (leaf 'shelters' produced by lerp insect grubs), sap (under peeling bark) and manna. *What's manna?* A sugary ooze produced by the leaves, fruit, buds and bark of some gums. These birds of a feather make dramatic autumn exits, with thousands rallying round prior to the big migration north.

WHITE-EARED HONEYEATER
Lichenostomus leucotis

 ACTIVE SUMMER

HABITAT
ACT • NSW • VIC

Ummm? Shouldn't that be the white-eared insecteater? Or perhaps the white-eared sapeater? By comparison with other honeyeaters, its beak is rather short. Perhaps that's why this honeyeater puts it to other uses, including lifting up bark and sucking snow gum sap. This loud cheeky bird also feeds on insects, beetles, ants and spiders tracked down under the leaves and bark of mature snow gums and spinning gums. Listen for its ringing *'cherrywheat'*, *'cherry-bob'*, *'chittagong'* and *'chock-chock-chock!'* sound effects.

SILVEREYE
Zosterops lateralis

☀ ACTIVE SUMMER

PHOTOGRAPH D WATTS / NATURE IOCUS

• white 'eye rings'

A summer blow-in, the silvereye feeds on insects, oozing lerp grubs, nectar, gum manna, shoots and twigs. Small flocks venture up to alpine heaths in search of insects and berries. At summer's end, with breeding over and done with, millions of silvereyes from as far south as Tasmania migrate by night along the ranges to Southern Queensland.

HABITAT

ACT • NSW • VIC

STRIATED PARDALOTE
Pardalotus striatus

PHOTOGRAPH D WATTS / NATURE IOCUS

SPOTTED PARDALOTE
Pardalotus punctatus

PHOTOGRAPH T A WAITE / NATURE IOCUS

☀ ACTIVE SUMMER

• both pardalotes 100–110 mm long

The commoner striated pardalote is the hardest to spot. Why? Because it's greenish, leaf-sized and blends in when feeding on lerps and insects on the outer canopy of snow gums. The striated pardalote prefers to nest in tree hollows. If they're in short supply, it makes do with an earthen bank burrow, the more likely nest site of its spotted relative. *Best time to see?* Autumn. That's when both species migrate through the Australian Alps in droves.

P.S. The pardalotes have similar 'paint jobs', except the striated pardalote is *spotless*.

P.P.S. The spotted pardalote keeps up a slow piping '*sleep-may-bee*' while the striated pardalote's call sign is a sharper double '*be quick*' and triple '*pick-it-up*'.

HABITAT

ACT • NSW • VIC

SUPERB FAIRY-WREN
Malurus cyaneus

☀ ACTIVE SUMMER

PHOTOGRAPH D WATTS / NATURE IOCUS

- if it's blue, it's male and breeding
- females & non-breeding males are drab brown
- brilliant territorial songsters

HABITAT

ACT • NSW • VIC

It's a good thing that feeding and tending fairy-wren youngsters is a *family affair*. The next generation fledge within two weeks of hatching, well before their tail feathers have developed. While they're on their flying 'L plates', the extended family rally round till the youngsters get the hang of it. There's method in group parenting, with the success rate of rearing offspring higher for *groups* than for couples.

P.S. Their brisk loud communal *'prip'* trill is not a throw away song. It's a jingle, advertising the fact that the territory is *occupied* and *defended*.

PHOTOGRAPH T & P GARDNER / NATURE IOCUS

FLAME ROBIN
Petroica phoenicea

☀ ACTIVE SPRING – SUMMER

- males flame-coloured chest & throat 'apron' and slate-black back & wings
- immatures & females drabber brown

HABITAT

ACT • NSW • VIC

One of the earliest birds to arrive in spring, the fidgety flame robin hunts and gathers in pairs. The twosome make short work of *snap-frozen* insects trapped on melting snowdrifts, including bogong moths. As the snows disappear, they stake out a patch of woodland. One's on the lookout, while the other prowls for worms and insects.

CRIMSON ROSELLA
Platycercus elegans

☀ ACTIVE ALL YEAR

PHOTOGRAPH C A HENLEY / NATURE IOCUS

What's *red and blue and eats with its mouth open*? This chirpy, gregarious bird is partial to snow gum nuts, mountain pea seeds, and the red berries of the alpine pepper and mountain plum pine.

P.S. Most juvenile rosellas are a motley olive-green but turn 'crimson' by their second birthday.

HABITAT

ACT • NSW • VIC

45

PHOTOGRAPH R. VALENTIC / NATURE FOCUS

HIGHLANDS COPPERHEAD
Austrelaps ramsayi

☀ ACTIVE SUMMER

Be afraid? Be respectful more likely, and reassured. For one, the highlands copperhead is rarely spotted. And while disturbing a 1.2 metre long snake in the grass (or bog) might come as a shock, this snake isn't eager to bite unless cornered or frightened. *Why waste energy and venom on a target too large to swallow when it can gulp down a frog or small lizard?* March is probably the worst month to encounter copperheads. That's when the female gives birth to 9–31 offspring.

HABITAT

ACT • NSW • VIC

RED-BELLIED BLACK SNAKE
Pseudechis porphyriacus

☀ ACTIVE SPRING – SUMMER

From above, you could confuse the copperhead with the 1.5 metre red-bellied black, but it lacks the vivid red belly. *Is it dangerous?* Absolutely, though it's more laid-back than the copperhead! *Where to see?* Down the mountain.

HABITAT

ACT • NSW • VIC

PHOTOGRAPH P. GERMAN / NATURE FOCUS

MAINLAND TIGER SNAKE
Notechis scutatus

☾ ACTIVE SPRING – SUMMER

HABITAT

ACT • NSW • VIC

PHOTOGRAPH P. GERMAN / NATURE FOCUS

The snake responsible for most human deaths in Australia is not very common in the Alps (*Phew!*) And because it's night-active in hot weather, your paths may never cross. In the colder months, it comes out by day to warm up, *so watch where you step.* If you spot one, best to back off calmly and allow it to slither off. *Favourite food?* Frogs and insects. *Average adult length?* 1.2 metres.

WHITE-LIPPED SNAKE
Drysdalia coronoides

🌙 ACTIVE SUMMER

HABITAT

ACT • NSW • VIC

The commonest alpine snake is also the *shortest* at 40 cm max. A decorative snake, its bite is painful but not deadly. Mostly night-active, it is sometimes spotted by day. *Where to see*? Anywhere small skinks—a favourite food—hang out. Live young are born in March in the lead up to winter, and three years pass before they're ready to go *solo*.

MOUNTAIN LOG SKINK
Pseudemoia entrecasteauxii

☀ ACTIVE SUMMER

• almost 10 cm long

Australia's highest dwelling reptile gets its middle name (log) from its favourite basking site in woodlands. Above the treeline, the lack of logs means that you're more likely to see the mountain *log* skink and friends (up to eight lizards per square metre!) draped over *bushes*

HABITAT

ACT • NSW • VIC

in the morning, and *boulders* in the afternoon. *Why the switch*? Initially too cold for comfort, as rocks warm up they become 'radiant heaters'.

MOUNTAIN SWAMP SKINK
Pseudemoia rawlinsoni

☀ ACTIVE SUMMER

Skinks tend to stick to quite narrow micro-habitats, for example swamps or tussocks. And although the 6 cm long mountain *swamp* skink might be found near the southern *tussock* skink and mountain *log* skink, they rarely trespass on each other's hunting grounds. That's because co-existence takes less energy than in-fighting. There's a possibility that this skink's 'gloss finish' scales assist slick getaways through the undergrowth if threatened. *How come*? Less friction!

HABITAT

ACT • NSW • VIC

ALPINE WATER SKINK
Eulamprus kosciuskoi

☀ ACTIVE SUMMER

PHOTOGRAPH P. GERMAN / NATURE FOCUS

Mostly found between 1400–2000 metres, the elusive alpine *water* skink likes damp settings including sphagnum bogs and wet heaths. Most common in NSW and ACT mountains, this flighty skink readily takes fright. *Where to?* It's thought they hole up in burrows excavated by crayfish and since vacated. *How to identify?* Dark stripes run along the length of this skink's 20 cm long olive brown body.

HABITAT

ACT • NSW • VIC

SOUTHERN WATER SKINK
Eulamprus tympanum

☀ ACTIVE SUMMER

• up to 23 cm long

HABITAT

ACT • NSW • VIC

PHOTOGRAPH T. MORLEY / NATURE FOCUS

PHOTOGRAPH G.LITTLE / NATURE FOCUS

The stouter southern water skink is most common along open rocky waterways. If you see one, you won't have to look far for the alpine water skink. The two species tend to cohabit in a relatively small patch, and engage in squabbling and chasing. Though living cheek by jowl, neither skink takes over the other's prime habitat, or food supply.

MOUNTAIN HEATH DRAGON
Tympanocryptis diemensis

☀ ACTIVE SUMMER

HABITAT

ACT • NSW • VIC

Egg laying is a risky reproductive strategy in the Alps as a cold snap could damage fragile eggs. Perhaps that's why these dragons prefer the sunnier north and west-facing slopes. The eggs start hatching in shallow burrows towards the end of February. A wait and see hunter, the dragon freezes if insects come near, catching them off guard with an extendable tongue.

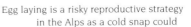

• 15 cm long lizard
• zig zag back stripes

SOUTHERN CORROBOREE FROG
Pseudophryne corroboree

ACTIVE SPRING – SUMMER

HABITAT

NSW

Not hopping, crawling! *How come?* Hopping isn't much use for a secretive species that lives under sphagnum moss for very good reason. It's too *obvious* for its own good, easily visible to keen-eyed predators.

Life's a bog There's little margin for error for a frog that only lays 26 eggs at a time. Add to that a life cycle that requires tadpoles to survive winter in a state of arrested development. Embedded in water-absorbing jelly, the 16 mm long 'taddies' await autumn and winter rains in their mossy nest chambers.

Getting enough moisture is one thing for a frog. Too much pollution is another, be it a silt or chemical overdose. Southern corroboree frogs were once quite common around Smiggin Holes in Kosciuszko National Park. Over the years, a combination of grazing activity, hydro-electric works, access roads and recreational activities have reduced and altered the frog's natural habitat.

Northern corroboree frog (*Pseudophryne pengilleyi*) With its slighter build and *lime-yellow stripes*, the northern corroboree frog population centres on the bogs of ACT's Namadgi National Park. Commoner than its southern lookalike counterpart, scientists hope it will be spared a dramatic shrinkage of range and numbers resulting from waterway pollution and habitat disturbance.

COMMON EASTERN FROGLET
Crinea signifera

ACTIVE SPRING – SUMMER

HABITAT

ACT • NSW • VIC

That *'crick crick crick'* heard around melting snowpatches and waterways may be a male froglet advertising its wares. The 'brand advertising' is pitched at potential female mates *and* male competitors. Since the females make their choice according to *something in the voice*, it's no wonder the froglets keep calling. As for male intruders, the cricking male is vocally warning them off its 'call site'.

49

ALPINE TREE-FROG
Litoria verreauxii alpina

☾ ACTIVE SPRING – SUMMER

HABITAT

NSW • VIC

Despite its name, the alpine *tree*-frog is actually an *earthbound* species. It's more at home around large pools, fens and wetlands in open valleys and high plains *above the treeline* where a whistling *'cree cree cree'* advertises its availability. Droughts in the early 1980s severely dented the once common tree-frog's population. Why? As pools dry up, tadpoles compete for scarce space, and fewer graduate to froghood. The alpine tree-frog is a high altitude subspecies of the whistling tree-frog (*Litoria verreauxii*) which occurs in the ACT, NSW and Victoria.

PHOTOGRAPH ACT PARKS & CONSERVATION SERVICE

BROWN TROUT
Salmo trutta

• around 30 cm long
  • few or no spots on tail fin

HABITAT

ACT • NSW • VIC

☀ ACTIVE ALL YEAR

What chance do native fish, frogs and 'taddies' have against a predator that can change colour to blend into its surrounds? An *unsporting one*, since this adaptation allows brown trout to steal up on unsuspecting prey. The introduction last century of rainbow and brown trout to the Alps rewrote the ecology of mountain streams and rivers. Over the past two decades, brook trout and Atlantic salmon have swelled the ranks of fishy 'outsiders'.

Introduced trout feed on beetles, caddis flies and moths, including large numbers of bogongs. In doing so, they directly compete for the food supply of the native mountain galaxias.

INTRODUCED
species

RAINBOW TROUT
Oncorhynchus mykiss

• less than 30 cm long
• spotted tail
• pink to red flush along head and sides

MOUNTAIN GALAXIAS
Galaxias olidus

 ACTIVE SPRING – AUTUMN

Since the introduction of trout, the last refuge for these 70–80 mm long native fish are the highest lakes and creeks—above the waterfalls and dams that thankfully bring migrating trout to a *'swimstill'*. Believe it or not, mountain galaxias are into *rock climbing*! They rely on water tension to slither and heave themselves up and over ledges. *Now why would a fish want to climb rocks?* Because on sunny days, rocks absorb heat, and are cosy-comfy to 'lounge around' on. Such 'warm up' climbs help galaxias to regulate their body temperature. *Amazing!*

HABITAT

ACT • NSW • VIC

SPINY CRAYFISH
Euastacus sp.

 ACTIVE SPRING – AUTUMN

HABITAT

ACT • NSW • VIC

Who made that burrow? The holes on the edges of bogs, streams and ponds are probably the claw-work of the spiny crayfish. Life hasn't been easy for this thick-skinned crustacean since foxes found their way to the high country. Prior to that, the cray's major predators were alpine water skinks and water rats. Sad to say, every bleached shell signals that another cray has been 'outfoxed'.

MOUNTAIN GRASSHOPPER
Acripeza reticulata

 ACTIVE SUMMER

HABITAT

ACT • NSW • VIC

While insects with shrunken or useless wings are less likely to be blown off the mountain during windy weather, they have problems making a quick exit. *So how does this clumsy flightless female grasshopper defend herself if caught out on daisy bushes and snow beard-heaths?* In short, bluff and bluster. To scare off attackers, she lifts her wings. *What's underneath?* Startling shades of red, black and blue. To some predators, the bold colour combination apparently signals danger—ie *eat me at your peril!*

insects • crayfish • fish

51

MOUNTAIN SPOTTED GRASSHOPPER
Monistria concinna

☀ ACTIVE SPRING – SUMMER

HABITAT

ACT • NSW • VIC

Come spring and these grasshoppers get the jump on other 'hoppers'. They're programmed to head for the light as soon as overlying snows begin to thin. *How do they tolerate -2 to -4°C winter temperatures?* Simple. They manufacture a chemical 'antifreeze' which prevents the mechanical damage that usually occurs when tissues freeze.

What do they eat? Up to 1.5 grams a day of alpine mint-bush leaves.

ALPINE THERMOCOLOUR GRASSHOPPER
Kosciuscola tristis

☀ ACTIVE SUMMER – AUTUMN

HABITAT

ACT • NSW • VIC

Why are so many alpine insects dark coloured? The darker the insect, the more solar energy they absorb when sunbasking. But temperatures change quickly in the Alps. Next to *icing up*, an insect's worst nightmare is *drying out*. That's why the alpine thermocolour grasshopper switches to a dark blue-green colour to improve heat intake when it's cold. If it's too hot, it reverts to a lighter green to avoid overheating. *How does the grasshopper change colour in the space of 2–3 hours?* It cleverly signals the brown and blue layers of granules in its outer 'skin' to *swap* places!

MACLEAY'S SWALLOWTAIL
Graphium macleayanum

☀ ACTIVE SPRING – SUMMER

HABITAT

ACT • NSW • VIC

Meet you at the top of the hill (with a view to mating lower down?) When butterflies gather on hilltops at certain times of year, they are taking advantage of *each other* rather than the superb views. Macleay's swallowtail, the commonest butterfly in the Australian Alps, is a noted 'hill topper'. It plays a key role pollinating plants, including the light-coloured flowers of the ovate phebalium and swamp heath.

BOGONG MOTH
Agrotis infusa

- Wing south
  September-October
- Wing north
  January-March

HABITAT

ACT • NSW • VIC

Each spring, millions of bogongs quit the lowland soils of northern NSW and south-east Queensland. Triggered by imminent food shortage, their annual journey to the Australian Alps is *high risk*! Countless thousands never make it there, let alone complete the return journey. *So why do they do it?* The immature moths have to slow down their maturation to keep in sync with their place of origin food supplies that dry up in summer, and revive the next autumn. Their necessary 'grow slow' requires a long spell in the refrigerator'—the Australian Alps.

Wind-assisted Prevailing winds sweep the moths south till they brush up against the mountains. Instinctively they home in on age-old hangouts in the highest rocky peaks. Packing into cool south and east-facing rock crevices, the moths form the densest of clusters—*up to 17 000 moths per square metre!*

Dusk exercise Each dusk and dawn, some of the moths stir. After vibrating their wings to warm up, off they dash in search of water and possibly nectar.

PHOTOGRAPH © ANIC IMAGE LIBRARY, CSIRO ENTOMOLOGY

PHOTOGRAPH © ANIC IMAGE LIBRARY, CSIRO ENTOMOLOGY

No rest for the exhausted Everyone wants a piece of this high-fat, nut-flavoured 'fast food', including little ravens, currawongs, and pipits. Mountain pygmy-possums, trout and reptiles also fatten up on the mass-produced moths that fly into the mountains each summer.

MARCH FLIES
Tabanus frogatti

 ACTIVE SUMMER

No *flies on you*? While small bush flies that coat one's back do little more than hitch a ride, there's a sting in the mouthparts of march flies from December till February. Unfortunately for bushwalkers, these flies survive the long cold winter in a state of suspended pupation just below the soil surface—ready to welcome spring (*and worry exposed skin!*)

HABITAT

ACT • NSW • VIC

NOT 'WINGING' IT

There's a good reason why many alpine insects are flightless. It gets around the 'Mary Poppins' factor ie 'have umbrella (or wings), will travel'. Because high winds are a feature of the mountain environment, insects that rely on flight to get around are likely to be carried some distance once airborne, and may end up in less suitable habitats that fail to supply their needs for food and shelter. Research suggests that around 60% of insect species which regularly venture above the tree line are unable to fly because their wings don't work, or they're wing-free.

KOSCIUSZKO METALLIC COCKROACH
Polyzosteria virridisima

 ACTIVE SUMMER

HABITAT

ACT • NSW • VIC

The heat-seeking behaviour of household cockroaches sees them clambering into home appliances. Alpine cockroaches also exploit all available heat sources. To maintain their preferred body temperature, they *shuttle* between sunpockets and shade. Their colouring, a bronze-brown to metallic green, allows them to absorb heat if exposed to sunlight. Look for them in windbreaks, especially amongst yellow kunzea heath.

PALEBROWN SAWFLY
Pseudoperga lewisi

☀ ACTIVE SUMMER – AUTUMN

PHOTOGRAPH C.A.HENLEY / NATURE IOCUS

HABITAT

ACT • NSW • VIC

Although their mothers must 'love' them, a writhing cluster of 'spitfires' (sawfly larvae) is not a pretty sight.

Why do they congregate? Cutting slits in snow gum leaves with her ovipositor, the female lays a clutch of eggs. They're looked after until old (*and ugly*) enough to fend for themselves. On maturing, they go to ground to pupate, and before long transform into the next batch of spitfires. **P.S.** Contrary to their name, sawflies are actually *wasps*!

ALPINE FUNNELWEB
Hadronyche meridiana

☀ ACTIVE SPRING – SUMMER

HABITAT

ACT • NSW • VIC

While this funnelweb's 'sting' isn't fatal, it is worth avoiding. To catch a meal, the spider sets up a silken 'sleeping bag' under a rock or log and lays out radiating trip wires. *Best (or worst?) times to see?* In spring, steer clear of agitated females flooded out of their burrows. They're the most painful. Also watch out for males clambering over the snowgrass in December, in search of females.

PHOTOGRAPH CLYDE O'DONNELL

PHOTOGRAPH CLYDE O'DONNELL

WOLF SPIDER
Lycosa species

☽ ACTIVE SUMMER

The wolf spider's burrow is its castle, hotly defended in alpine herbfields and grasslands. Look for the raised entrance of web and plant matter which may help keep out snow or water. Over winter, the hole is sealed over with a thick sheet of silken webbing. We suggest you Do Not Disturb!

HABITAT

ACT • NSW • VIC

Introduction to Australian Alps
PLANTS

As altitude increases, the lower temperatures, frosty conditions, greater exposure to cold winds, and a shorter growing season make it increasingly difficult for trees to absorb enough solar energy to grow trunk and roots. As their energy intake decreases, they become increasingly stunted, and eventually give up at the tree line. Above this cut-off point, a mosaic of low-growing plant communities makes up the ground cover.

Adopting a low profile is a clever strategy in windswept alpine tracts, with many plants sheltering behind rocky outcrops and more robust vegetation. Draping over bare ground or boulders brings an added bonus during the snow-free months. Carpet-like plants benefit from the heat absorbed by the rock surfaces. And low profile plants have less to squash when the snow arrives, suffering fewer branch breakages.

At higher altitudes, the growing season has to be squeezed in between snow melt and the all-too-rapid return of the snow clouds. High country plants use a variety of growth and reproductive strategies to increase their chances of survival and spread from year to year. These include shooting from underground roots or sprouting from seeds which overwinter beneath the snow. Because the growing season is unusually short and subject to frosts and snap snowfalls, many alpine plants have little to show for the year's effort. In the most exposed zones, annual growth may be measured in millimetres.

Despite seemingly tough living conditions, from December till March the alpine and subalpine meadows host magnificent floral displays. Organic soils built up over long periods of time on the rolling landforms encourage a diverse prolific flowering.

Please note, the flowering times indicated for each plant *are a guide only*. They can vary from year to year by a matter of weeks or months, depending on the altitude of the actual plant in question, and its degree of shelter. For example, a snow daisy growing in a sheltered subalpine location is likely to start flowering before one growing in an exposed alpine location. Another complicating factor is the severity of the preceeding winter. A long harsh winter with heavy snowfalls depresses the start of flowering, while a lighter snow cover usually triggers a quick-off-the-mark flowering season.

Changes afoot? Because of an on-going review of plant classification, the scientific names of some plants found in the Australian Alps have been changed in the past decade, or will be in the near future. The most up-to-date names at the time of publishing have been used.

MOUNTAIN ASH
Eucalyptus regnans

- all trunk, tiny crown
- long ribbons of shed bark
- usual height range 55–75 metres

HABITAT

VIC

With tallest specimens passing the 100 metre mark, Victoria's mountain ash runs a close second to the world's tallest tree, the giant Californian redwood. *Why so tall and straight?* Questions would be asked if they weren't! Everything's going for them, including the best growing conditions in the Alps. *Which are?* Sheltered slopes, heavy year round rainfall, and moist fertile soils enriched by recycled leaf litter nutrients.

P.S. *'Regnans'* comes from the latin *regnare* (to rule)—entirely apt for Australia's tallest tree.

PHOTOGRAPH K DILETTI / NATURE FOCUS

TOWERING INFERNOS

Unlike most eucalypts which resprout after fire, alpine and mountain ash literally can't take the heat. With their dangling bark ribbons encouraging wildfires to 'burn them to death', before long it's ashes to ashes. *What's their comeback?* Between fires, they produce vast numbers of seeds, many of which crack open when burnt, sprouting en masse in the nutrient-rich ashbed. That's why you come across plantation-like same age stands of both types of ash, rather than the usual mixed eucalypt forests.

How to tell the two ash apart? Trunks of mature mainland alpine ash are usually half rough-barked (with longitudinal furrows) and half smooth (with insect scribbles). Mountain ash are more likely to have a 'stocking' of fibrous rough bark at the base (up to 15 metres) giving way to a greenish grey bark. Mountain ash have smaller crowns than alpine ash.

ALPINE ASH
Eucalyptus delegatensis

- medium-sized crown
- top half smooth & scribbled.
- usual height range 20–40 metres

HABITAT

ACT • NSW • VIC

Although the tallest alpine ash overlook the forest floor from a height of 90 metres, there's not much to look down on. *Why?* Because so little light filters through the ash canopies, the undergrowth is spartan—shade-loving ferns and soft-leaved shrubs. *How to pick alpine ash from a distance?* The new spring growth flushes a bright red, clearly visible just below the subalpine zone.

PHOTOGRAPH COLIN TOTTERDELL

57

PHOTOGRAPH COLIN TOTTERDELL

BROWN BARREL
Eucalyptus fastigata

- average 30–45 metres
- massive trunk around 60% of total height
- long hanging bark strips

HABITAT

ACT • NSW • VIC

A long 'stocking' of rough fibrous bark covers the trunk—hence the name 'brown'—finally giving way to smooth white upper limbs. Peaking at 60 metres, brown barrel usually occurs in gullies and on cool slopes. While it sometimes grows in pure stands, it's also found in the company of mountain and alpine ash, mountain and ribbon gum, and the peppermints. Look out for old stubs on the trunk. *Once were branches!*

CANDLEBARK
Eucalyptus rubida

- average height 10–40 metres
- lance-like mid-veined leaves

HABITAT

ACT • NSW • VIC

Candlebarks strike a sentinel-like pose in open forests and woodlands on tablelands and mountain slopes. Look for a reddish bark ruff around the base of the 'candle'. The rows of dark marks (like giant fork prongs) scoring the white trunk are the handiwork of burrowing insects. In summer the white bark turns reddish, which is where the Eucalyptus gets its *'rubida'* (ie ruby-redness).

PHOTOGRAPH COLIN TOTTERDELL

PHOTOGRAPH COLIN TOTTERDELL

MOUNTAIN GUM
Eucalyptus dalrympleana

- average height 40–60 metres

HABITAT

ACT • NSW • VIC

Slimmer and shorter than the mountain and alpine ash, the mountain gum grows in mixed company, and features an open untidy crown. A colourful tree, it sports a metre high 'sock' of rough grey bark which gives way to a smooth yellow-white blotchy bark. In summer, the bark turns colourful shades of olive green, pink and red.

RIBBON (MANNA) GUM
Eucalyptus viminalis

HABITAT
ACT • NSW • VIC

How to tell the mountain gum from the lookalike *ribbon gum*? If practical, check the young leaves. Mountain gum juveniles are *rounded* and deep green, compared to the ribbon gum's pale green *dagger-like* leaves. There's another way to distinguish if you've got binoculars. Look for suck marks on the ribbon gum's trunk. Yellow-bellied gliders regularly tap into the sap and 'fill up' on the sticky nutrients.

PHOTOGRAPH COLIN TOTTERDELL

PHOTOGRAPH CLYDE O'DONNELL

NARROW-LEAVED PEPPERMINT
Eucalyptus radiata subsp. *robertsonii*

• 10–30 metres height
• grey or brownish bark

HABITAT
ACT • NSW • VIC

While both peppermints have rough-barked trunks and branches, it is easy to tell them apart. As their names suggest, it's all to do with *leaf width*! While the adult leaves of both are up to 15 cm long, the width of the broad-leaved peppermint is 7 cm max compared to the narrow-leaved peppermint's 1.5 cm. Broad or narrow, crush either leaf for a *minty tang* of the essential oils, cineole and piperitone. Reaching that leaf shouldn't be hard as peppermints have low slung, drooping branches.

PHOTOGRAPH CLYDE O'DONNELL

BROAD-LEAVED PEPPERMINT
Eucalyptus dives

• 20–25 metres height
• dark grey-brown bark

HABITAT
ACT • NSW • VIC

BLACK SALLY
Eucalyptus stellulata

HABITAT
ACT • NSW • VIC

Why 'black' when its smooth oily bark is usually striped yellow, olive green or pinkish brown? It's probably because the rough bark covering half the trunk is dark grey to grey-black. And from a distance, its overall dark colouring sets it apart from the lighter snow gum or 'white sally'. This upright gum prefers wetter high country sites, fringing stream banks and frost hollows, and needs a downpour to bring out its true colours.

PHOTOGRAPH CLYDE O'DONNELL

59

trees

PHOTOGRAPH COLIN TOTTERDELL

SNOW GUM
Eucalytpus pauciflora

Toeing the tree line Australia's
toughest tree? When it comes to
cold-tolerance, the evergreen

HABITAT

ACT • NSW • VIC

- 10–20 metres high tree, often sprawling
- white creamy-grey, smooth bark, often 'scribbled'
- 18 cm long glossy, blue-green adult leaves with parallel veins

snow gum surely wins hands down. But even snow gums pull up short at the tree line where the *woodlands* of lower altitudes are reduced to snow gum *shrublands*. It's not suprising that the gums become more stunted and twisted the higher they grow. Decades of fierce winds and frosts force the gums into contorted shapes. Snowed under and iced up for around four months a year, there's many a snow-smothered branch that snaps under the weight.

P.S. In other parts of the world, subalpine trees are either hardy conifers, or deciduous (losing their leaves for the winter).

P.P.S. In autumn and winter, alpine snow gums de-bark, revealing a mix and match of pinkish-red bark that eventually bleaches to cream.

Shoot from the roots Spare a thought for snow gums caught in the firing line. The fire-sensitive, thin-barked gum shoots from the roots, resulting in a multi-branched 'mallee' growth habit. Bushfires leave a tangled mess of recovering woodland in their wake, and probable eviction (or worse) for animals that rely on hollow limbs and trunks—be they possums or parrots.

Frozen food For vegetarian wildlife, snow gums provide a year round supply of gumnuts, leaves and sap. This allows some animals to overwinter rather than migrate to lower altitudes for alternative food supplies.

RADIATA PINE
Pinus radiata

HABITAT

ACT • NSW • VIC

In *its place*, this Californian import has its pluses. A quick grower, it's a good source of plantation softwood timber, and forms sturdy windbreaks. BUT, its robust nature and speedy growth are problematic when seeds *stray* into mountain woodlands and forests.

PHOTOGRAPH COLIN TOTTERDELL

BLACK CYPRESS
Callitris endlicheri

- 5–20 metre tree
- coarse-furrowed, dark reddish-brown bark

HABITAT

ACT • NSW • VIC

'*The pine clad ridges raised on high?*' The conifer made famous in 'The Man from Snowy River' was the black cypress. The dark green, cone-shaped tree is mostly found on drier mountain ridges, often in drier 'rainshadow' areas. Like all cypresses, its needles are made up of minute scale-like leaves (2–4 mm long). Look for its dark brown globular 'cones' (2 cm diameter) which contain lots of small, winged seeds.

BLACKWOOD
Acacia melanoxylon

FLOWERS SPRING – SUMMER

- small shrub to 35 metre tree
- 7–12 cm long leaves

HABITAT

ACT • NSW • VIC

One of Australia's tallest wattles, the blackwood shares well-watered mountainous slopes with ribbon gum and mountain ash. *What to look for?* A mass of pale yellow wattle 'balls', long coiled seed pods, and 3–7 lengthwise leaf veins on its broad 'leaves'.

P.S. Outside conservation reserves, blackwood is regarded as one of the world's best furniture timbers.

PHOTOGRAPH D GREIG © ANBG

BLACK WILLOW
Salix nigra

HABITAT

ACT • NSW • VIC

Aaaah! That choking sensation is what mountain streams and banks experience when black willows invade their space. Very pretty, yes, but very welcome, no—*and certainly not in national parks*. One of three invasive introduced woody weeds, the fast growing, deciduous black willow (dark grey bark) grows to 20 metres, and has been making a nuisance of itself since arriving from North America in 1962 (*Worst luck!*).

SILVER WATTLE
Acacia dealbata
FLOWERS SPRING

PHOTOGRAPH CLYDE O'DONNELL

- dark brown to black bark
- large shrub to a medium-sized tree
- favours gullies & mountain slopes

HABITAT

ACT • NSW • VIC

Tiny white hairs give this wattle's feathery 'leaves' a silvery look. Like all wattles, *it thrives on disturbance*, colonising ground that's been burnt or cleared. The wattle's 'long life' seeds remain dormant in the soil until they're fired into life. That's why you often find same age stands of wattle growing up thick and fast. But there's a comedown to their *come uppance* in the long run. Insects, fungi and mistletoe parasites thin their ranks.

VICTORIAN CHRISTMAS BUSH
Prostanthera lasianthos
FLOWERS SPRING – SUMMER

- up to 4 metres tall
- finely toothed, 4–8cm 'lance' leaves

HABITAT

ACT • NSW • VIC

Look out for this tall bushy shrub when driving up or down the mountains. W*here*? In cool moist shady gullies on a twist or bend in the road. If you can pull off safely, crush a leaf and sniff! Yes, it's a *'mintie'*, a close relative of the alpine mint bush. The glorious spots and splodges on its lopsided flowers aren't just for decoration. They're landing signals for potential insect pollinators, signalling *touch down here!*

PHOTOGRAPH COLIN TOTTERDELL

DUSTY DAISY–BUSH
Olearia phlogopappa

FLOWERS SPRING – SUMMER

HABITAT

NSW • VIC

Preferring rocky sites and heaths, the spectacular dusty daisy-bush is well equipped for alpine life. That's because its rigid, silvery-grey leaves don't wilt during temporary water shortages. Nor are they damaged if the shrub is buried 'alive' beneath the snow.

ALPINE DAISY-BUSH
Olearia algida

FLOWERS SPRING – SUMMER

Who's been plucking this daisy's petals? Mother Nature, it seems.

HABITAT

ACT • NSW • VIC

Its tiny rigid leaves actively practice water conservation. *How come?* The smaller the leaves, the fewer the water exit routes (or stomates)—very important during the hotter months.

SNOW BEARD-HEATH
Leucopogon montanus

FLOWERS EARLY SUMMER

HABITAT

ACT • NSW • VIC

Where's the beard? If your eyesight is up to it (or you've got a magnifying glass), check inside the tiny tubular flowers for ... *a big disappointment*. It's the only Alps beard-heath that's 'close-shaven'! A tough wiry shrub, the snow beard-heath varies in height from mere centimetres in feldmarks to a 60 cm shrub in more sheltered areas.

P.S. The related mountain beard-heath is true to its name—*hairy throated. Where to see?* Snow gum woodlands, and on mountain slopes.

SWAMP HEATH
Epacris paludosa

FLOWERS SPRING – SUMMER

- 6–10mm leaves
- 5mm long floral tubes

HABITAT

ACT • NSW • VIC

In keeping with European heaths, Australian Alps heaths are hardy, small-leaved shrubs with the ability to thrive on poor, damp soils. A dense, bushy shrub up to a metre high, the prickly swamp heath is the tallest heath above the tree line. It thrives in watercourses and boggy wet bouldery sites.

flowering shrubs & herbs

CORAL HEATH
Epacris gunnii
FLOWERS EARLY SUMMER

- 0.5–1 metre high shrub
- rigid chunky oval leaves
- 4–6mm wide flowers

PHOTOGRAPH COLIN TOTTERDELL

If you trained a weatherproof, time release camera on this heath *for several decades*, you'd be able to watch it 'go walkabout' across the windswept feldmark. *How does the heath shift location?*

HABITAT

ACT • NSW • VIC

The wind-driven heath dies off on the exposed side, and grows in the lee, its stems edging forward just 10 mm a year. By this process it *travels*, creating a shifting patchwork of heath and bare ground. In more sheltered positions, it manages to reach shrub status.

ALPINE BAECKEA
Baeckea gunniana
FLOWERS SUMMER

- grows to 2 metres
- 2–4mm leaves
- 4–5mm wide flowers

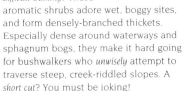

HABITAT

ACT • NSW • VIC

Think baeckea, think difficult walking! These aromatic shrubs adore wet, boggy sites, and form densely-branched thickets. Especially dense around waterways and sphagnum bogs, they make it hard going for bushwalkers who *unwisely* attempt to traverse steep, creek-riddled slopes. A *short cut*? You must be joking!

PHOTOGRAPH COLIN TOTTERDELL

PHOTOGRAPH © MURRAY FAGG ANBG

WOOLLY TEA-TREE
Leptospermum lanigerum
FLOWERS EARLY SUMMER

- shrub to 5 metre tree

Which bits of this tea-tree are woolly? The young fruit and buds. *Where to see?* Mountain gullies and wet forests—especially along waterways. The leaf length of the woolly tea-tree is highly variable, varying from 8 mm at lower altitudes through to 18 mm higher up.

HABITAT

ACT • NSW • VIC

OVATE PHEBALIUM
Nematolepis ovatifolium
FLOWERS SUMMER

HABITAT
NSW • VIC

- 0.5–1 metre high aromatic shrub
- 1 cm diameter flowers with pinkish-red buds
- glossy oval leaves

Rumour has it that bogong moths break their summer fast to *top up* on the phebalium's energy-rich nectar. There's plenty to go around as it's one of the commonest shrubs above the tree line, particularly in heaths and rocky areas. Its tough, spreading branches set up a deceptively solid carpet over rocks and boulders, and *pitfalls galore* for 'rockhopping' walkers venturing off track.

ALPINE MINT-BUSH
Prostanthera cuneata
FLOWERS SPRING – SUMMER

- 0.5–1.5 metre high shrub
- 10–15 mm long white to pale mauve flowers

HABITAT
ACT • NSW • VIC

Those in the know would recognise this common heath shrub blindfolded, *especially if they stepped on it by mistake* (which isn't encouraged!) The foliage gives off a delightful minty aroma. And *don't insects just love it?* Peer into one of the flowers. Those markings aren't random. Apparently the dainty dots and splotches guide insects onto the flowers' flattened 'landing pad'. And into contact with the *all important pollination zone.*

CARPET HEATH
Pentachondra pumila
FLOWERS SUMMER

- 4–12 cm high 'mats' up to 1 metre across
- stiff shining leaves up to 6 mm long
- crimson 'berries' 6–8 mm diameter

HABITAT
NSW • VIC

Bright green leaves, red fruits and white woolly flowers? This ground hugger lays down an ornamental 'carpet' too pretty to tread on. The green fruit bide their time beneath the snows and ripen early in summer. Look for it in heaths, tall alpine herbfields, tussock grassland and exposed feldmark.

flowering shrubs & herbs

PHOTOGRAPH COLIN TOTTERDELL

WHITE SPEEDWELL
Derwentia derwentiana
FLOWERS SUMMER

- 3–10 cm pairs of toothed, lance-like leaves
- up to 1 metre high perennial

Expect to encounter this sprawling herb in moist, shaded forests. Look for its dainty branched 'candelabra' made up of 20 cm high, white to pale lilac 'candles'.

HABITAT

ACT • NSW • VIC

BLACKBERRY
Rubus discolor

INTRODUCED
species

FLOWERS SPRING – SUMMER

- red-black tasty fruit

HABITAT

ACT • NSW • VIC

Surely the one redeeming feature of this rambling European import is its autumn crop of blackberries? Unfortunately not. The bad news is that blackberry seeds pass through birds and other animals unharmed, ready to start up a new infestation. That's why blackberries are out of control in many parts of the Australian Alps, including mountain forest gullies, along waterways, and anywhere the landscape has been *disturbed by other uses.*

CASCADE EVERLASTING
Ozothamnus secundiflora
FLOWERS SUMMER – AUTUMN

- 0.5–2 metre high shrub
- sticky grey, hairy oblong leaves
- tiny flowerheads (4–6 mm)

Don't expect to find this spicy everlasting beside a cascade or creek. The 'cascade' refers to its *arching branches.* Clustered with dense, creamy white flowerheads, they give a vague impression of 'white water'. A common shrub in snow gum woodlands, the everlasting shrinks with increasing altitude, sheltering behind boulders and other bushes.

HABITAT

ACT • NSW • VIC

COMMON CASSINIA
Cassinia aculeata
FLOWERS SUMMER – AUTUMN

PHOTOGRAPH BARBARA CAMERON-SMITH

This 'irritating' aromatic plant seems to thrive on disruption. That's why its showy clusters of creamy, crowded flower-heads are such a common sight along roadsides, or on exposed rocky outcrops. Leaf length separates common cassinia (3 cm leaves) from its relatives. The long-leaf cassinia's leaves are up to 10 cm long. *Best not to go measuring up the leaves* as they can irritate sensitive skins.

• 2 metre high bushy shrub

HABITAT

ACT • NSW • VIC

ALPINE EVERLASTING
Ozothamnus alpinus
FLOWERS SUMMER – AUTUMN

HABITAT

NSW • VIC

• shrub grows to 1 metre high

The miniature 'bouquets' of white flowers that stud this shrub look like 'starbursts', with each flower supported by striking, reddish modified *leaves*.

PHOTOGRAPH COLIN TOTTERDELL

INTRODUCED
species

YARROW
Achillea millefolium
FLOWERS SPRING – AUTUMN
Here's a European import that mostly sticks to a special category of habitat—mountain roadsides (disturbed ground)! *Shut your eyes as you drive past.* It's the only way to eradicate yarrow—or milfoil as it's also known—from view, at least in the short term.

HABITAT

ACT • NSW • VIC

67

ANENOME BUTTERCUP

Ranunculus anemoneus

FLOWERS SPRING – EARLY SUMMER

- grows to 35 cm high
- flowers 4–6 cm diameter

HABITAT

NSW

PHOTOGRAPH COLIN TOTTERDELL

One of the *world's largest buttercups* begins to bud the moment light penetrates the pitch-black world beneath the snowpack. Look for its stunning flowers near snowpatches and snowmelt streams, alpine herbfields or shady rock crevices. *Once common*, it has made a spectacular comeback since livestock grazing was phased out of Kosciuszko National Park. Recorded on Mount Hotham in 1887 (*but no longer*), the species was already under threat from stock grazing.

SILVER SNOW DAISY

Celmisia astelifolia

FLOWERS SUMMER

HABITAT

ACT • NSW • VIC

PHOTOGRAPH COLIN TOTTERDELL

If conditions are right, this most endearing of alpine plants flowers so extensively and enthusiastically that from a distance, it could be mistaken for lingering snow patches. The very presence of these tall snow daisies (up to 50 cm high with 5 cm wide flowers) indicates that fertile, moist, well-drained soils lie below. *Best place to see*? Above the tree line in the company of snowgrass. *Where does the 'silver' come from*? Look closely at the stems, leaves and fruits. The silky *insulating* hairs are responsible for the *silvery* grey sheen.

SILKY SNOW DAISY

Celmisia sericophylla

Found only in Victoria, the larger silky snow daisy doesn't mind wet feet, springing up below sodden snow patches in cool sheltered valleys.

SNOW DAISIES

Bracyscome spp.

FLOWERS SUMMER

PHOTOGRAPH COLIN TOTTERDELL

With too many species to mention by name, the *smaller-flowered* alpine snow daisies (20 mm flowerheads) take a backseat to the more spectacular silver snow daisy. They grow vigorously after snowmelt around rocks and melting snow patches, adding colour and movement to their surrounds. As their 'flowers' vary from white to lilac, it's been a toss-up where to include them in this guide, *colour wise*.

HABITAT

ACT • NSW • VIC

HOARY SUNRAY
Leucochrysum albicans
FLOWERS SUMMER

Firmly anchored by a creeping woodstock, this 'everlasting' crops up in short alpine herbfields and the wind-blasted rocky feldmark. *Check out its 'survival kit'.* The woolly hairs covering stems and leaves provide insulation in sub-zero temperatures. They also *reflect* solar rays during the parched summer months, reducing water loss. And because its white bracts (petal look-alikes) are *stiff* and papery, sunray flowerheads maintain a brave face where softer petals might wilt.

P.S. Below the alpine zone, hoary sunrays adopt an *all-yellow scheme*—the bracts included!

ALPINE MARSH-MARIGOLD
Caltha introloba
FLOWERS SPRING

This game little marigold actually buds and blooms beneath the snow. *Brrr! How does it know when to spring to life?* As soon as light starts to filter through thinning snows. The light-sensitive marsh-marigold resumes growth long before most other plants break their dormancy. In pitch dark, these 'icebergs' draw on energy stored in roots and stems the previous season. *Where to see?* In short-lived streams or on rocky meltwater slopes—anywhere it's icy cold, and wet, wet, wet!

CLOVERS
Trifolium spp.
FLOWER SPRING – AUTUMN

INTRODUCED species

There's bound to be a four leaf amongst them, but we wish all clovers *good riddance* rather than good luck! The two you're most likely to see along roadsides and vehicle tracks in the Alps are the crimson clover and white clover. Both were introduced to Australia to improve imported pastures (and *infest* native grasslands!). *Why do they thrive in the mountains?* Probably because there's no shortage of water.

flowering shrubs & herbs

69

flowering shrubs & herbs

ALPINE GENTIAN
Chionogentias mulleriana
FLOWERS SUMMER

HABITAT

ACT • NSW • VIC

Who cares that the gentians Heidi so admired in the Swiss Alps are a lot more spectacular than our modest 'crocuses'. *Keep your eyes peeled late summer* for these 'pyjama-striped,' creamy-yellow petals in damper grasslands. The three to four cup-shaped flowers seem an overly heavy load for those thin purplish stems.

PHOTOGRAPH COLIN TOTTERDELL

GLACIAL EYEBRIGHT
Euphrasia collina subsp. *diversicolor*
FLOWERS SUMMER

PHOTOGRAPH COLIN TOTTERDELL

Which *eyebright is that*? Good question. A number of species *brighten the eye* in the damper parts of alpine herbfields. This one stages massed displays in snowmelt areas. While it's all sweetness and light above ground, these perennial herbs get a nutritional leg up from neighbouring plants. *How so*? They link up via specialised underground roots and tap in, which means they're semi-parasites— *pretty ones at that.*

HABITAT

NSW

MAUVE LEEK ORCHID
Prasophyllum suttonii
FLOWERS SUMMER

- 15–30 cm high stems
- 6–8 mm long petals

HABITAT

ACT • NSW • VIC

Talk about confusing! A more accurate name would be the purple-flecked white leek-orchid. Watch where you tread when crossing alpine herbfields and boggy areas. The sweet-smelling orchid can be hard to spot if you're too busy admiring the view.

PHOTOGRAPH COLIN TOTTERDELL

ALPINE SUNDEW
Drosera arcturi
FLOWERS LATE SUMMER

HABITAT
ACT • NSW • VIC

PHOTOGRAPH COLIN TOTTERDELL

How *can this plant thrive in water-logged, nitrogen-deficient sites?* Simple. The bog-bound sundew has an independent supply of essential nutrients—*insects!* Bedazzled by the gland-tipped hairs fringing each leaf, curious insects are in for a sticky reception if they touch down. Movement-sensitive trigger hairs bend over, trapping the unlucky insect. Its life juices, including the all important nitrogen supplement, are slowly *digested*.

MUD PRATIA
Pratia surrepens
FLOWERS SUMMER

PHOTOGRAPH COLIN TOTTERDELL

This dainty 'mud wrestler' always looks clean, despite its preference for boggy habitats. A creeping plant of fens, bogs and tussocks, the mud pratia has been practicing soil conservation for thousands of years. Eh? That dense mat of well-anchored, spoon-shaped leaves hold an 'umbrella' over the soil, minimising loss to high winds, heaving ice needles and heavy rain.

P.S. The flowers vary from *white to bluish* in colour.

HABITAT
NSW • VIC

WHITE PURSLANE
Neopaxia australasica
FLOWERS SUMMER

HABITAT
ACT • NSW • VIC

PHOTOGRAPH COLIN TOTTERDELL

This trans Tasman herb varies its leaf size to suit the habitat. At higher altitudes, it's a mat-forming creeper, colonizing the toughest of niches. 'Lawns' of vivid green 1–2 cm leaves take over water-logged, semi-bare ground vacated by snow patches. At lower altitudes in swamps and running water, the leaves balloon to 10 cm in length. In the aftermath of high country livestock grazing, the purslane's patch-up skills were recruited by soil conservationists to revegetate eroded alpine slopes in Kosciuszko National Park.

PHOTOGRAPH COLIN TOTTERDELL

MOUNTAIN CELERY
Aciphylla glacialis
FLOWERS EARLY SUMMER

- 30–70 cm herb
- dark green, leathery leaves

HABITAT

NSW • VIC

This robust 'celery' is hard to overlook in tall alpine herbfields. While *showiness* helps attract insect pollinators, it had drawbacks when cattle and sheep grazing was in full swing each summer. Fortunately the fleshy herb staged a successful comeback from a tough underground rootstock. Its less conspicuous relative, the mountain aciphyll, (found in Namadgi National Park) was also eaten *out of its habitat* by cattle.

SILVER EWARTIA
Ewartia nubigena
FLOWERS SUMMER

HABITAT

NSW • VIC

At first glance, 'Australian edelweiss' (as ewartia used to be called) is a rather plain *mat* of a plant, forming silvery grey hummocks in tall alpine herbfields. But looks aren't everything in the plant world. Over time, it casts a heavy duty 'tarpaulin' over some of the toughest rocky sites in the Australian Alps—the notorious feldmark zone—*shielding thin soils*. Close up, the 'bonsai' flowerheads are charming. *Get down on your knees* for a good look at the tiny, white, papery flowerheads surrounded by pinkish bracts.

PHOTOGRAPH COLIN TOTTERDELL

PHOTOGRAPH COLIN TOTTERDELL

ALPINE GREVILLEA
Grevillea australis
FLOWERS SPRING – SUMMER

HABITAT

ACT • NSW • VIC

This grevillea adopts a range of habits, varying from rockdraping to upright (2.5 metre high), mostly on damp ground or near swamps. As their *unshowy* spidery floral clusters (4–6 mm *across*) are *light*-coloured and strongly *scented*, they may attract *night-flying* moth pollinators rather than day-active insects. Look for oblong leaves up to 12 mm long.

TALL RICE FLOWER
Pimelea ligustrina
FLOWERS SUMMER

- 2.5–4 cm flowerheads
- shrub to one metre high
- 10–15 mm reddish bracts

HABITAT

ACT • NSW • VIC

You can hardly blame high country graziers for nicknaming this spectacular rice flower the 'Kosciusko Rose'. While it looks rose-like from a distance, the large reddish 'petals' are actually *bracts*, enclosing tiny, creamy white flowers studded with yellow stamens. Because these 'roses' lack *thorns*, it's a fair bet that livestock grazing heaths above the tree line dined out on the tall rice flower.

CANDLE HEATH
Richea continentis
FLOWERS SUMMER

- 2–3.5 cm crowded leaves
- multi-branched shrub to 1 metre high
- 5–10 mm long clustered flowers

HABITAT

ACT • NSW • VIC

Take our word for it—this low profile shrub is best admired from a distance. That's not only because it tends to congregate on boggy ground. The sheathing leaves spiralling around the reddish stem are *prickly*! Look for its 'candles' of creamy, white flowers in and around sphagnum bogs.

ALPINE STACKHOUSIA
Stackhousia pulvinaris
FLOWERS SUMMER

HABITAT

NSW • VIC

Such a big scent for such a little plant, by night and day! *No wonder it's also known as the scented star-flower.* The much-branched perennial forms dense cushions or mats of crowded, bright green leaves.

Where to smell its delightful fragrance? Try moist sites, including tussock grasslands and tall alpine herbfields. At lower altitudes, the related candles (*Stackhousia monogyna*) bear aloft 10 cm long creamy flower spikes.

73

ALPINE PEPPER

Tasmannia xerophila

FLOWERS SUMMER

- shrub to 1.5 metre high
- 5–8 mm wide, purplish black berries
- 7–10 mm leaves

PHOTOGRAPH COLIN TOTTERDELL

HABITAT

ACT • NSW • VIC

What's the advantage of having peppery leaves? A hot mix of chemicals might help reduce the amount of leaves lost to insect munching. The more leaves spared, the more energy the plant has available for photosynthesis. Are the red stems a warning to insects? Possibly. **P.S.** Look out for the related mountain pepper (T. *lanceolata*) in shady mountain forests.

ALPINE ORITES

Orites lancifolia

FLOWERS SUMMER

HABITAT

ACT • NSW • VIC

Do the creamy white flowers remind you of anything? Orites (pronounced or-EYE-teez) belongs to the same family as grevilleas (Proteaceae family) and has a similar response to bushfires. Their boat-shaped seed pods crack open when heated, releasing the next generation in the form of winged seeds.

PHOTOGRAPH COLIN TOTTERDELL

PHOTOGRAPH COLIN TOTTERDELL

ALPINE BOTTLEBRUSH

Callistemon pityoides

FLOWERS SPRING – SUMMER

- leaves up to 2.5 cm
- flowering spikes up to 5 cm

HABITAT

ACT • NSW • VIC

Each creamy yellow bottlebrush is a massed 'bouquet' of tiny flowers, overflowing with showy stamens. Where to find this shrub which can grow up to three metres high? Anywhere that's damp underfoot, including sphagnum swamps and mountain watercourses.

YELLOW KUNZEA
Kunzea muelleri
FLOWERS SUMMER

- shrub up to 1 metre
- 3–7 mm incurved leaves
- leaves dotted with glands

HABITAT

ACT • NSW • VIC

This sunny little shrub forms extensive sprawling dwarf heaths, often around boggy areas and in partnership with epacris heaths. The dainty yellow flowers feature five petals and a showy fizz of overhanging yellow stamens.

PHOTOGRAPH COLIN TOTTERDELL

ALPINE WATTLE
Acacia alpina
FLOWERS SPRING

- 1–1.5 metre high erect shrub

Wattles have successfully colonized most of the continent, but only one—alpine wattle—has ventured into the tough alpine zone. Despite its resilience, you are more likely to spot the short flowering wattle spikes in subalpine woodlands. And what look like leaves are actually flattened 2–4 cm long stems (phyllodes).

HABITAT

ACT • NSW • VIC

PHOTOGRAPH COLIN TOTTERDELL

MOUNTAIN HICKORY WATTLE
Acacia obliquinervia
FLOWERS SPRING – SUMMER

HABITAT

ACT • NSW • VIC

Ranging from a large shrub to a 20 metre tree, this widespread wattle has a smooth grey bark. Its false leaves (phyllodes) vary between 5–15 cm long and 1–4.5 cm wide.

PHOTOGRAPH A MCWHIRTER © ANBG

BUFFALO SALLOW WATTLE
Acacia phlebophylla
FLOWERS SPRING

HABITAT
VIC

While the Buffalo sallow wattle is quite common on Mount Buffalo's granite plateau, you won't find it anywhere else in the whole wide world. It is one of a trio of 'exclusive to Mount Buffalo' plants, including the Buffalo sally *Eucalyptus mitchelliana* (a type of snow gum), and the fern-leaf heath myrtle *Baeckea crenatifolia*. All three were probably *once more widespread* in surrounding foothill and range country. *What shrunk their distribution?* Rising temperatures and falling rainfalls across Australia may have gradually marooned these surviving *endemics* on the cool, wet mountain outcrop.

PHOTOGRAPH CLYDE O'DONNELL

HABITAT
ACT • NSW • VIC

ENGLISH BROOM
Cytisus scoparius
FLOWERS SPRING

Exploding pods? What a clever way to scatter broom seeds. But since this broom was introduced to Australia in the early nineteenth century, few have applauded its efficient rate of spread. Certainly not Australian Alps national parks staff who struggle to control broom outbreaks. To make matters worse, the seeds of this naturalised shrub *hitch a ride* on mud-spattered vehicles, footwear, horses, passing wildlife and waterways, *taking root* wherever they come to rest.

Want the really bad news? An estimated 20 000 seeds per square metre of soil bide their time around every broom bush. If only we could make a clean sweep of such ... *weeds!*

INTRODUCED
species

PHOTOGRAPH COLIN TOTTERDELL

LEAFY BOSSIAE
Bossiaea foliosa
FLOWERS SPRING – SUMMER

• 5–10 mm hairy seed pods

HABITAT
ACT • NSW • VIC

Sure is leafy! Masses of tiny chunky leaves smother each branchlet of this upright shrub that grows to a metre high. Come spring and the wiry shrub transforms itself—and entire hillsides—from green to lemon yellow. Check out its 'crown jewels'—the flattened seed pods—that go to ground and patiently await resurrection.

TWIGGY MULLEIN
Verbascum virgatum

FLOWERS SPRING – AUTUMN

INTRODUCED
species

Introducing (*and not without regret*) twiggy mullein. Standing up to 2.5 metres high, this hardy European escapee sadly stands out in any crowd of native wildflowers and flowering shrubs. W*here*? Roadside and other *disturbed* areas.

HABITAT
ACT • NSW • VIC

ST JOHN'S WORT
Hypericum perforatum

FLOWERS SPRING – SUMMER

- 2.5 metre high perennial stems
- egg-shaped fruit capsules

HABITAT
ACT • NSW • VIC

INTRODUCED
species

It's a shame this native of Eurasia and Northern Africa didn't stay put in its home territory, *regardless of its reputed medicinal qualities*. Disturbed areas are prime targets for this hard-to-eradicate weed which readily takes root in the foothills and lower Alps, often along waterways. St John's *wart* more likely!

ALPINE SHAGGY PEA
Podolobium alpestre

FLOWERS SUMMER

- hairy seed pods
- 10–12 mm long pea flowers

Look for clusters of orange-*yellow* pea flowers with orange-*red* keels.
Expect to see this tough, wiry sprawling *'bacon and eggs'* shrub in an upright or reclining position, depending on the local conditions, with leaves up to 4 cm long.

HABITAT
ACT • NSW • VIC

PHOTOGRAPH COLIN TOTTERDELL

flowering plants

77

PHOTOGRAPH COLIN TOTTERDELL

GRANITE BUTTERCUP
Ranunculus graniticola
FLOWERS EARLY SUMMER

- up to 20 cm high stems
- 15–25 mm diameter flowers
- toothed leaves

HABITAT

ACT • NSW • VIC

This clumpy yellow buttercup is one of many native to the Alps. It's fairly common in the tall alpine herbfields and tussock grasslands. *How to identify?* Check out the ultra gloss petals. Perhaps the shiny petals draw insect attention on the same principle as lost walkers flashing shiny objects at search planes. There's another distinguishing feature to keep in mind. Some granite buttercups have 'black eyes' (or centres)!

GUNN'S ALPINE BUTTERCUP
Ranunculus gunnianus

HABITAT

NSW • VIC

PHOTOGRAPH COLIN TOTTERDELL

DANDELIONS
Taraxacum sp.
FLOWERS SUMMER – AUTUMN

HABITAT

ACT • NSW • VIC

Talk about spreading itself too thickly. *The worst place to see?* Along roads and vehicle tracks throughout the mountains, anywhere where horses, livestock, vehicles and people have roamed, past and present. *How did they get there?* Their seeds hitched a ride, either inside animals, or on vehicles, or the belongings of passers-by.

NATIVE YAM

Microseris lanceolata

FLOWERS SPRING – SUMMER

- 10–40 cm high herb

PHOTOGRAPH COLIN TOTTERDELL

HABITAT

ACT • NSW • VIC

The native yam was highly sought after by Aboriginal people who made annual trips to the high country. Like a buoy marking a submerged diver, the yellow flower signalled buried 'treasures'— up to 10 small fleshy cylindrical roots. *Yum!* Roast native yam.

VARIABLE GROUNDSEL

Senecio lautus

FLOWERS SUMMER

PHOTOGRAPH COLIN TOTTERDELL

HABITAT

ACT • NSW • VIC

- 4–8 cm long rosette leaves

This daisy's bright yellow flowers presumably evolved over millions of years to attract insect pollinators. But for over a century of high country grazing, groundsels were targetted by cattle and sheep. It's no surprise that they've bounced back in areas where grazing has ceased. *Where to find this herb which can grow to 40 cm high?* Around rock outcrops and boulders.

IVY-LEAF GOODENIA

Goodenia hederacea subsp. *alpestris*

FLOWERS SUMMER

- 2–3 cm diameter round, toothed leaves

HABITAT

ACT • NSW • VIC

This perennial creeps like ivy over exposed surfaces, including open gravelly ground. Mainly found in subalpine tracts, the goodenia's close-pressed, glossy leaves protect soils from driving wind and rain. Flowers 15–20 mm diameter.

PHOTOGRAPH COLIN TOTTERDELL

flowering shrubs & herbs

79

ALPINE PODOLEPIS
Podolepis robusta
FLOWERS SUMMER
• *20–40 cm* high

HABITAT

ACT • NSW • VIC

It's not the neatest of plants. Each flowerhead consists of a *hub* of central disc florets (tiny flowers) surrounded by *spokes* of sparse raggard ray florets. Most common below the tree line, it was nicknamed 'mountain lettuce' by graziers because of its rosette of broad crinkly leaves.

CLUSTERED EVERLASTING
Chrysocephalum semipapposum
FLOWERS SPRING – SUMMER

HABITAT

ACT • NSW • VIC

Instead of single bobbing 'buttons', this daisy produces clusters of small flowerheads (10–20 in all), borne on stems which range from 30–60 cm. The narrow leaves are *sticky* to the touch.

BILLY BUTTONS
Craspedia spp.
FLOWERS SUMMER

HABITAT

ACT • NSW • VIC

Hey, what happened to this daisy's petals? Have they blown off or what? Billy buttons are *petal-free* daisies held aloft on a slender stem. Each nodding yellow 'button' is actually a bunch of tiny flowers (disc florets). Look for an untidy rosette of leaves at ground level. Leaf shapes and sizes are the best ways to identify different types of billy buttons. *Any idea what role the soft fuzzy coating on stems and leaves plays?* The hairs help insulate the plant in cold weather, and reflect sunlight in summer.

SCALY BUTTONS
Leptorhynchos squamatus
FLOWERS SUMMER

- herb up to 25 cm
- leaves up to 3.5 cm in length flowerheads up to 30 mm diameter

These 'polka dot' flowerheads brighten up tussock grasslands and tall alpine herbfields. *Check under the leaves.* They wear white 'woollies' year round.

HABITAT

ACT • NSW • VIC

BUTTON EVERLASTING
Helichrysum scorpioides
FLOWERS SUMMER

HABITAT

ACT • NSW • VIC

Everlasting? Yes. *Button?* Not when compared to billy buttons. A perennial herb, this daisy's papery flowerheads sit on top of 15–25 cm high stems. *Leaves?* Soft green and hairy.

GOLDEN EVERLASTING
Bracteantha subundulata
FLOWERS SUMMER

HABITAT

ACT • NSW • VIC

- up to 60 cm high plant
- leaves 13 cm long

The papery flowerheads are certainly durable. While the shining 'petals' lose their intense hue as winter approaches, they never wilt. In fact, faded 'flowers' are sometimes seen poking through thin snow. The 8 cm wide flowerhead consists of a 2.5 cm diameter disc of tubular orange *true* flowers, surrounded by golden yellow modified leaves (or bracts).

flowering shrubs & herbs

MOUNTAIN CALADENIA
Caladenia lyalli
FLOWERS SPRING – SUMMER

HABITAT

ACT • NSW • VIC

PHOTOGRAPH COLIN TOTTERDELL

This dainty 'pink hood' gives the impression that it has something to hide. *Perhaps it has.* The flowering spikes of 1–4 flowers (steely white inside) were apparently a welcome sight for Aboriginal people who dug for its small fleshy roundish tubers—a popular vegetable —during the warmer snow-free months.
Where to find this 10–30 cm high herb? Boggy sites.

ALPINE BORONIA
Boronia algida
FLOWERS SUMMER

PHOTOGRAPH COLIN TOTTERDELL

HABITAT

ACT • NSW • VIC

If you know your boronias from lower altitudes, you'll recognise the distinctive white to deep pink flowers and sweet aroma. The 4–6 mm flowers have four petals, and the leaflets are 3–5 mm long. This twiggy bush keeps a low profile on rocky or gravelly ground.

ALPINE RICE–FLOWER
Pimelea alpina
FLOWERS SUMMER

• 10–15 mm diameter flowerheads

HABITAT

NSW • VIC

One of the handful of sweet-scented mountain plants, the alpine rice-flower is a multi-branched perennial which produces pink to creamy white flowerheads. Look out for this dainty sprawler in alpine heaths, especially around low rocks and boulders. It also crops up underfoot in alpine grasslands, *so watch where you tread!*

PHOTOGRAPH COLIN TOTTERDELL

GRASS TRIGGER PLANT
Stylidium graminifolium
FLOWERS SUMMER – AUTUMN

HABITAT

ACT • NSW • VIC

PHOTOGRAPH COLIN TOTTERDELL

Talk about ingenious! As the name suggests, the flower has a spring-loaded trigger which catapults forward if brushed by an insect. *Evolution gone mad?* Not at all. Coated with pollen, the insect sets off in search of the next trigger plant. On landing, the pollen 'dust off' unwittingly spreads fresh pollen dust from plant to plant. *Where?* Grassy and boggy areas.

PHOTOGRAPH COLIN TOTTERDELL

GUNN'S WILLOW–HERB
Epilobium gunnianum
FLOWERS SUMMER

If you spot an upright, pink-flowering herb in earshot of trickling water, there's a good chance it's the Gunn's willow-herb. This moisture-loving perennial thrives in seepage areas around boulders, or near bogs and streams.

- 10–15 mm long petals
- 10–70 mm high herb

HABITAT

ACT • NSW • VIC

MOUNTAIN CORREA
Correa lawrenciana
FLOWERS SUMMER

HABITAT

ACT • NSW • VIC

These 2–3 cm long 'tubular bells' brighten up sheltered, high rainfall mountain forests. To avoid confusion, keep in mind that it's not unusual at lower altitudes to find the same species in flower, *minus the cheery band of red.* Usually 1–3 metres high, the shrub features 2–6 cm long, opposite leaves.

PHOTOGRAPH CLYDE O'DONNELL

flowering shrubs & herbs

PHOTOGRAPH COLIN TOTTERDELL © ANBG

ROYAL GREVILLEA
Grevillea victoriae
FLOWERS SPRING

- 1–2 metre understorey shrub

Talk about pulling power! The quick-off-the-mark flowering of this grevillea prompts honeyeaters to fly in well before the snow disappears. They're in for a right royal welcome—copious supplies of nectar, readily accessed by their slim tapering beaks. When the flowering finishes, the honeyeaters make a quick exit.

P.S. Botanists are in the process of splitting this 'super' species into a number of different species, *so scientific name changes are afoot*.

HABITAT

ACT • NSW • VIC

SHEEP SORREL
Acetosella vulgaris
FLOWERS SPRING – SUMMER

INTRODUCED
species

- spear-shaped leaves

HABITAT

ACT • NSW • VIC

Soil conservationists rolled out an unintentional *red carpet* when they covered damaged alpine ranges with bitumen, hay and chicken wire to protect what was left of precious topsoil. Seeds of the sheep sorrel, a native of Eurasia, came with the hay. Decades later, flowerheads of tiny reddish flowers still spring up on disturbed areas.

INTRODUCED
species

BIDGEE-WIDGEE
Acaena novaezelandiae
FLOWERS SPRING – SUMMER

- 15–20 cm flowering stems
- 2 cm diameter flowerheads

HABITAT

ACT • NSW • VIC

Keep your burrs to yourself! A sprawling perennial herb, bidgee-widgee forms dark green patches up to a metre wide in damp grasslands and tall alpine herbfields. The greenish, globular, flowerheads are unmistakeable, as are the plentiful supply of spiny seed cases which attach themselves to passing objects, *including wildlife and walkers' socks*!

MOUNTAIN PLUM-PINE
Podocarpus lawrencei
FRUITS SUMMER

HABITAT

ACT • NSW • VIC

Here's one ground-hugging shrub that rarely show its age. In alpine zones, a metre wide plum-pine might be several hundred years old, *its annual growth measured in millimetres.*
Over thousands of years, this slow-growing shrub has given other plants a start in life. *How come?* As it 'millimetres' over barren screes and bare ground, the plum-pine sends down roots, fostering the build up of soil and moisture. Less hardy plants take advantage of this pioneer plant's groundwork, and the shelter it provides in a tough habitat.
P.S. Look out for the plum-pine's red 'fruit'.

SCOTCH THISTLE
Onopordum acanthium
FLOWERS SUMMER

INTRODUCED
species

HABITAT

ACT • NSW • VIC

If only one could give the national emblem of Scotland the *caber toss* once and for all. Unfortunately it has proved to be a stayer in its adopted country, sprouting in parts of the Alps previously used for pasture. Other introduced thistles with potential to harm the high country include the spear thistle and nodding thistle, which both hail from Africa and Eurasia.

ROUND-LEAF MINT BUSH
Prostanthera rotundifolia
FLOWERS SPRING

• up to 4 metre high bush
• 5–10 mm rounded leaves

HABITAT

NSW • VIC

It's worth driving through the Alps in spring, if only to catch a glimpse of this splendid bush, awash with masses of 10 mm wide lilac-purple flowers. *Where?* Along shady creeks and rivers, or around rocky outcrops. For a 'rocky mountain high', drink in the heady mint aroma, especially if you're tired. According to aromatherapy, peppermint is good for *concentration* (and perking up tired drivers?).

flowering shrubs & herbs

ALPINE HOVEA

Hovea montana

FLOWERS SPRING

- purple to light mauve flowers
- sprawling wiry shrub to 40 cm high

This vivid pea shrub can hardly wait for the snow to melt before it bursts into flower. Its sweet-smelling flowers attract a buzz of insects to snow gum woodlands and grassy slopes. Just to complicate matters, you'll sometimes come across a 'whitewashed' version, with its pea flowers lacking colour.

P.S. The undersides of the shiny green 30 mm long leaves could do with a shave. *Check out the rusty hairs!*

HABITAT

ACT • NSW • VIC

PHOTOGRAPH COLIN TOTTERDELL

EYEBRIGHT

Euphrasia collina subsp.*diversicolour*

FLOWERS SUMMER

HABITAT

NSW

A late flowerer, this widespread eyebright favours drier sites in tussock grassland, tall alpine herbfields and heaths. Look for its large showy flowers in shades of violet, lilac or white.

PHOTOGRAPH COLIN TOTTERDELL

PHOTOGRAPH COLIN TOTTERDELL

SHOWY VIOLET

Viola betonicifolia

FLOWERS SUMMER

- herb up to 10 cm high
- flowers up to 15 mm across

You'll find this widespread native violet in tall alpine herbfields and tussock grassland (*and lots of suburban cottage gardens!*) Talk about adaptable. The sweet-scented flowers range from deep violet to pale purplish-white, with darker veins. *Leaves?* Up to six cm long and shaped like a spear head.

HABITAT

ACT • NSW • VIC

HEBE

Chionohebe densifolia

FLOWERS SPRING – SUMMER

- dense, thick overlapping leaves
- up to 10 cm high shrub

HABITAT

NSW

Growing in tandem with coral heath helps this delicate-looking hebe to maintain a toehold in the tough feldmark zone. The heath's woody branches provide a windbreak of sorts. *Where to see*? The choice is limited (unless you're heading to New Zealand's alps). Try the western edge of Kosciuszko's Main Range between Mount's Lee and Twynam.

SKY LILY

Herpolirion novae-zelandiae

FLOWERS SUMMER

- 2–6 cm long grassy leaves
- pale lilac-blue to white flowers

HABITAT

ACT • NSW • VIC

What a shame these glorious 10–12 mm diameter flowers are so *short-lived*. You'll be lucky to find sky lilies above the tree line, but keep an eye out in damp alpine herbfields. Subalpine woodlands are a better bet. Minus their flowers, patches of the sky lily could easily be mistaken for a fine *grassy lawn*.

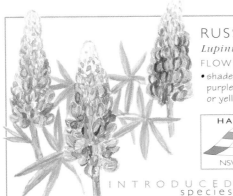

RUSSELL LUPIN

Lupinus hybrid

FLOWERS SUMMER

- shades of blue, purple, pink, white or yellow

HABITAT

NSW • VIC

INTRODUCED species

'*How lovely!*' visitors exclaim. The half a metre high pea flower spikes are indeed spectacular, dwarfing less obvious peas native to the Australian Alps. Sadly this European ornamental is an *escapee* from ski resorts and mountain villages, rapidly spread by seed.

VIPERS BUGLOSS
Echium vulgare

FLOWERS SUMMER – AUTUMN

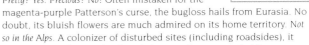

Pretty? Yes. Precious? No! Often mistaken for the magenta-purple Patterson's curse, the bugloss hails from Eurasia. No doubt, its bluish flowers are much admired on its home territory. *Not so in the Alps.* A colonizer of disturbed sites (including roadsides), it can be very hard to shake once it gets a toehold. Undeterred by heights, it's found up to 2100 metres.

INTRODUCED species

TASMAN FLAX-LILY
Dianella tasmanica

FLOWERS & FRUITS SUMMER – AUTUMN

Surely one of the satin bowerbird's favourite plants, the blue flax lily produces a marvellous crop of violet-blue flowers, offset by bright yellow anthers. Its deep green berries ripen to the same striking blue, brightening rocky sites in snow gum woodlands and damp forest gullies. *Why 'flax'?* Its long, sheathed leaves are reinforced by strong, silky leaf fibres, similar to the New Zealand flax cultivated in the Pacific Region for fibre and berries.

WAXY BLUEBELL
Wahlenbergia ceracea

FLOWERS SUMMER – AUTUMN

- 2–3 cm long leaves
- 6–9 mm long sky blue flower tube

What a refreshing sight—sky blue native bluebells nodding in damp alpine grasslands, and along stream banks. If you spot a *deep blue-violet* version, don't dismiss it as an oddity. More likely, it's the royal bluebell. *So much for the regal name.* The royal bluebell is more likely to be found at *lower* altitudes than the waxy bluebell, especially in snow gum woodlands.

ROYAL BLUEBELL
Wahlenbergia gloriosa

FLOWERS SUMMER

ALPINE LEEK ORCHID
Prasophyllum alpinum
FLOWERS SUMMER

HABITAT

ACT • NSW • VIC

This rather drab greenish-brown orchid plays second fiddle to its larger showier relative, the mauve leek-orchid. They're often found in each other's company, around bogs and mossy beds. It's worth getting down on hands and knees for a quick sniff. M*m-mm!* That 'come hither' scent surely makes up for this leek-orchid's camouflage colouring. Stand back. H*ere come the insects!*

TWO-FLOWERED KNAWEL
Scleranthus biflorus
FLOWERS SPRING – SUMMER

HABITAT

ACT • NSW • VIC

Here's one of a number of Australian Alps natives that have made the big leap from the wilds to the rock garden. The stiff leaves

of this tufted perennial herb form 'crew cut' cushions or mounds 10–20 cm in diameter. The tiny green-paired flowers are anything but conspicuous. The 2.5 mm flowers are lacking in size *and petals.* Look for the knawel on damp slopes, mainly below the tree line.

HARD CUSHION PLANT
Colobanthus pulvinatis
FLOWERS SUMMER

HABITAT

NSW • VIC

S*often that cushion?* Not if the cushion plant wants to survive. Only the most robust, streamlined plants can cope with life on the windward edge of mountain ranges. Stiff rigid leaves are a plus in short alpine herbfields and exposed feldmark zones. So is a tough root system tapping deep into thin stony soil and anchoring the cushion. It also prevents the plant being heaved out of the soil by ice needles. The related alpine colobanth provides a much *softer* 'cushion' but we'd prefer you didn't put either to the test.

PINEAPPLE GRASS
Astelia alpina
FLOWERS SPRING – SUMMER

HABITAT

NSW • VIC

If you're thinking of stretching out on the mountain tops, make sure you don't get the *raw end of the pineapple* grass (or silver astelia). Those lance-like silvery leaves are definitely not sandal-friendly. W*here to*

see? This tufted perennial forms dense rosettes on the edges of sphagnum bogs, and in autumn is likely to bear a crop of glossy black berries.

flowering shrubs & herbs

89

ALPINE TUFT-RUSH
Oreobolus pumilio

• leaves bright green and up to 25 mm long

HABITAT

ACT • NSW • VIC

If you come across a *donut-shaped* tufty plant in boggy areas, it's probably a tuft-rush. The flattened leaves usually form cushions or extensive carpets a few centimetres high. But if the cushions die off in the middle while the edges keep growing, the end result might be a 30 cm diameter ring. *Where to see?* Along the margins of fens and streams, and in short alpine herbfields.

TUFTED SEDGE
Carex gaudichaudiana

• 20–40 cm high sedge
• 25 mm brown male spikelet

HABITAT

ACT • NSW • VIC

This drab-looking alpine sedge has played a very important time-keeping role in the Australian Alps. *How so?* Widespread and common, the tufted sedge forms dense peats, the oldest known dating back 15 000 years. This timeframe helped scientists to work out that glaciers must have retreated by that date. In their wake, pioneering plants like the tufted sedge were in the process of recolonising the barren mountains. Look for the sedge's stiff grass-like leaves (2–4 mm wide) in shallow water, pond margins and damp hollows.

SPHAGNUM MOSS
Sphagnum cristatum

These lime green 'sponges' are vital water controllers in the Alps. *Their job?* Making sure that rainfall in general (and

HABITAT

ACT • NSW • VIC

snowmelt in particular) is absorbed and gradually released, especially throughout summer. Prior to high country grazing, spongy moss carpets, *metres thick*, naturally occurred in damp areas. Burnt off to reduce the risk of horses and other livestock stumbling into mossy pitfalls, its water-storage capacity was likewise reduced. *Oh, for the benefit of hindsight.* **P.S.** The mosses' framework allows other herbs and shrubs to get a start in life.

SOFT TREE-FERN
Dicksonia antarctica

HABITAT

ACT • NSW • VIC

This glorious understorey fern thrives in moist gullies because the latter offer the shelter and moisture required for optimal fern growth and reproduction. Look for the tell-tale trunk up to five metres tall, matted with rusty root-hairs. The gracefully arching fern fronds can reach three metres in length. *Best time to see?* With a dusting of snow. *Pure magic!*

PHOTOGRAPH R BLAKERS / NATURE IOCUS

PHOTOGRAPH COLIN TOTTERDELL

MOTHER SHIELD-FERN
Polysticum proliferum

- grows to 20–60 cm above tree line
- 100 cm high at lower altitudes

HABITAT

ACT • NSW • VIC

Like all ferns, this widespread species can't do without water. Why? Its mode of reproduction requires a 'swimming leg' in order for the male gamete and female ovum to meet up. To survive hot dry spells, it reduces water loss by sheltering among rocks, sprouting from cool crevices. Look for large fronds covered with long, brown, hairy scales.

ALPINE WATER-FERN
Blechnum penna-marina

HABITAT

ACT • NSW • VIC

Widespread above the tree line, especially along streams in tall alpine herbfields, this fern puts out long, wiry, creeping rhizomes.
In season, a red-brown mass of spore cups can be seen on the underside of its fronds (up to 40 cm long).

PHOTOGRAPH © MURRAY FAGG ANBG

SNOW GRASSES
Poa spp.

It is no coincidence that grasses are so widespread above the tree line. Tussocks crop up in mountainous regions the world over because they're cold climate specialists.

How come? Dead or alive, grass leaves insulate and protect new growth at the base of the tussock. *Protection from what?* For starters, ice needles (frozen water between soil grains) that heave poorly anchored plants from their life support system—the soil.

P.S. *What do snowgrasses have in common with human hair?* They're both *dead* at the ends but *alive* near the base.

PRICKLY SNOW GRASS
Poa costiniana

PHOTOGRAPH COLIN TOTTERDELL

• up to 80 cm high

Why *prickly?* Try the lie-down test, and you'll soon discover that its bright green, shining leaves are coarser and stiffer than those of other snowgrasses. A widespread hardy alpine snowgrass, it is partial to damp sites, including tussock grasslands, fens, bogs, streamsides, and damper parts of tall alpine herbfields.

SOFT SNOW GRASS
Poa hiemata

This snowgrass is a *soft touch*, as its name suggests. Common in tall alpine herbfields, the delicate grass grows to 15–60 cm in height and features very fine soft, smooth hair-free leaves. *Leaf colour?* A shining green—at least while alive! It usually grows in the company of the prickly snow grass on moist alpine slopes. But before you take a seat, it's not easy to pick the *soft* from the *prickly* at a glance.

PHOTOGRAPH COLIN TOTTERDELL

ALPINE WALLABY-GRASS
Austrodanthonia nudiflora

- 10–40 cm high

HABITAT

ACT • NSW • VIC

What to look for? Stiff, sharp shining leaves (2–15 cm long), and straight stems. *Where?* Tussock grasslands, fens and damper parts of tall alpine herbfields. It often grows in the company of snow wallaby-grass which features delicate leaves up to 10 cm long, and masses of shining reddish stems.

RIBBONY GRASS
Chionochloa frigida

- 45–120 cm high tussocks
- smooth, shining stems

HABITAT

NSW

Exclusive to Kosciuszko National Park, this giant alpine grass forms metre wide, glistening tussocks on steep rocky slopes and along watercourses. A hardy perennial, it thrives on bare, sloping soils. Pushed to the brink of extinction in the 1930s, it has regrouped since the phasing out of summer grazing. Given half a chance, *it is a long-life grass*, with larger tussocks up to a *hundred years old!*

KANGAROO GRASS
Themeda triandra

HABITAT

ACT • NSW • VIC

Once widespread throughout Australia, the fate of this native grass was sealed once livestock began to graze its edible young growth. Annual high country grazing resulted in kangaroo grass being eaten out in the foothills. *Where to see these remnant reddish grasses?* Mainly along roadsides, and in fenced off sheltered locations. The tufted perennial grass produces flowering stems over a metre high, but early reports that the latter could be tied over the horse's saddle were probably *exaggerated.*

index

Some Useful Reading

For more detailed information on the Australian Alps, look out for the following books in national park visitor centres, specialist bookshops (natural history museums and botanic gardens) or your local library.

- ACT Parks and Conservation Service, 1993. *Wild About Canberra: A Field Guide to the Plants and Animals of the ACT*, ACTPCS, Canberra.

- Australian Alps Liaison Committee, 1998, *Explore the Australian Alps - Touring Guide to the Australian Alps National Parks*, New Holland Publishers (Australia), Sydney.

- Australian Alps Liaison Committee, 1999, *Australian Alps Walking Track Map Guide* 2nd edn. Australian Alps Liaison Committee, Canberra.

- (The) Australian Museum, 1983, *Complete Book of Australian Mammals - The National Photographic Index of Australian Wildlife*, by R Strahan (ed), Angus & Robertson Publishers, Sydney.

- Barrow, G, 1995, *Exploring Namadgi & Tidbinbilla - Day Walks in Canberra's High Country*, 2nd edn, Dagraja Press, Canberra.

- Cogger, H G, 1996, *Reptiles & Amphibians of Australia*, 5th edn Reed Books Australia, Melbourne.

- Costin, A B, Gray, M, Totterdell, C J & Wimbush, D J, 1979, *Kosciusko Alpine Flora*, CSIRO/Collins Australia, Sydney (reprint in process)

- Flood, J, 1996, *Moth Hunters of the Australian Capital Territory - Aboriginal Traditional Life in the Canberra region*, J M Flood, Canberra.

- Fraser, I & McJannett, M, Fitzgerald, H (illust) 1998, *Wildflowers of the Snow Country - A Field Guide to The Australian Alps*, Vertego Press, Canberra ACT.

- Gowland, K and Slattery, D, (eds) 1992, *Australian Alps Education Kit*, Australian Alps Liaison Committee, Melbourne.

- Green, K & Osborne, W, 1994, *Wildlife of the Australian Snow-country - A comprehensive guide to alpine fauna*. Reed Books, Sydney.

- Hadlington, P W & Johnston, J A, 1990, *An Introduction to Australian Insects*, New South Wales University Press, Sydney.

- Lamp, C, & Collett, F, 1996, *Field Guide to Weeds in Australia*, 3rd edn, Inkata Press, Melbourne.

- McCann, L R, 1996, *The Alps in Flower*, 3rd edn, Victorian National Parks Association Inc, Melbourne.

- Morecombe, M, 1986, *The Great Australian Birdfinder - Where and how to find Australian Birds*, Weldon Publishing, Sydney.

- Readers Digest, 1976, *Complete Book of Australian Birds*, Readers Digest Services Pty Ltd, Sydney.

- Sainty, G, Hoskings, J & Jacobs S (eds) 1998, *Alps Invaders - Weeds of the Australian High Country*, Australian Alps Liaison Committee, Canberra.

- Siseman J, 1993, *Alpine Walking Track : Walhalla to Canberra*, 2nd edn, Pindari Publications, Blackburn, VIC.

- Slattery, D., 1998, *Australian Alps - Kosciuszko, Alpine and Namadgi National Parks*, UNSW Press, Sydney.

- Taylor, M & Canberra Ornithologists Group, 1992 *Birds of the Capital Territory - An Atlas*, National Capital Planning Authority, Canberra.

- Triggs, B, 1984, *Mammal Tracks and Signs - A Field Guide for South-eastern Australia*, Oxford University Press, Melbourne.